Sisters of the Sole (Soul)

Created and Written
By
Janie Van Komen and Lyn Austin

Copyright 2014

ISBN: 978-0-9716237-8-1

Other Works by Janie Van Komen

The Opa Legacy
Sarah Jane's Very Best Story Ever
Beyond Beauty

email:jvkwriter@aol.com

www.janievankomen.com

Other Works by Lyn Austin

Carol of the Heart
The Auction
The Quiet Storm

www.romancenovelsbylyn.com
email: lynmaupin@yahoo.com

This book is licensed for your personal enjoyment only. This book may not be copied or reproduced without written permission from either Janie Van Komen or Lyn Austin. The information and opinions in this book do not in any way supercede the advice of counselors, or medical practitioners. And it makes no claims other than those of personal opinion.

Dedication

We dedicate this book to our mothers:
Barbara Wood Buchanan, and **RowaneThomas Westergard,**

who as **Soul Sisters,**
supported, sustained, and uplifted each other
through life and death, heartaches, and heartbreaks,
through the happy times of celebration and the joys this life offers to all.
They were our inspiration, encouragement,
and our cheerleaders for this project.

Table of Contents

	Page
Chapter 1 - Cleaning Out the Shoe Closet	7
Chapter 2 - Clean the Mud off my Shoes…	17
Chapter 3 - If I buy Athletic Shoes will I be an Athlete?	29
Chapter 4 - What do You Think of My Shoes?	37
Chapter 5 - Wearing Slippers to Shop is Tacky	49
Chapter 6 - Get Out of the Shoebox	55
Chapter 7 - I Shouldn't have Spent that Much Money on Shoes!	65
Chapter 8 - Want New Shoes? Make a List	81
Chapter 9 - Wear the Soft Soled Shoes	91
Chapter 10 - What if I Walk Backwards, Turn Around 3 times, and Wear Purple Shoes?	103
Chapter 11 - I Dare You to Wear that Pair of Shoes.	115
Chapter 12 - So What if Your Shoes get Wet	129
Chapter 13 - Take the Shoes from Off Your Feet	139
Chapter 14 - I Love These Shoes!	153
Chapter 15 - I Want Shoes That Fly!	165
Chapter 16 - End of Day, Shoes off, Feet up, Rest…	175

Sisters of The Sole (Soul)

Chapter 1 - Cleaning Out the Shoe Closet

Open the shoe closet door to the low level explosion of worn-outs, blister making, too loose, too tight, one missing, not matched, flip flops stuck in the tops of winter boots, straps are broken, out of style, mess before your eyes... In other words open up a chaotic out-of-control shoe closet and Zap! your energy level just dropped three notches.

Open your eyes every day to a chaotic out-of-control life closet and Zap! just climbing out of bed can send that same energy level south of the border.

We are here to help you sort things out, clean things up, and discard the junk cluttering your life closets. We know your energy level will rise, your attitude will change, and you will be happier.

What is the definition of an energy-zapping life closet?

Answer: Any person, place, pair of shoes, or situation you currently deal with in your life, and wish it were somehow different.

Janie:

Years ago my cousin, Robyn, and I were running a few errands. The operative word here was 'running.' Congested lives, atypical trials, and other circumstances, forced crowding momentary pleasures into random routine kid runs from point A to point B. I waited in the car with the babies. Robyn dashed into a store, and purchased a pair of shoes she had seen on sale earlier that week. We were on the road again in fifteen minutes flat.

Arriving at Robyn's house I helped carry her younger children and the travel trappings inside. Husband, Scott, had picked up the older children half an hour ago and was now pacing in front of the window. Checking his watch as we walked in he let us know he did not want to be late for his meeting. Robyn pulled the newly purchased shoes out of the box and presented them before her husband with the flair of a caravan merchant approaching the Sultan.

"Scott," she said, "look at my new shoes, (pause), aren't they great? (pause), I just love them!"

With the expertise of a game show model she lifted up the shoes displaying the details.

Scott turned back long enough to dispel the "men don't pay any attention myth" and a smile curled under his mustache. Carefully he articulated each word.

"Robyn, please tell me you did not actually pay money for those shoes."

At that exact shoe exhibition moment Cameron hit Zachary with a toy and took off running around the room making squealing pig noises every time Zachary got within retaliation distance. Three-year-old Whitney tipped over the glass of milk she had begun pouring. With the milk still dripping off the edge of the countertop, Molly, the dog, jumped into the spreading floor puddle. All four paws splatted the milk into a greater mess. The dog lapped at the white pool in an effort to help Whitney clean up the spill.

Without raising an eyebrow, flinching a muscle, or seeming to be aware of the immediate chaos raging around her, Robyn, every bit as gifted as those ancient caravan merchants, raised the shoes once again. She caressed the toes lightly with her finger and said, "You know, Scott, sometimes buying a pair of shoes is the only thing in my life I have any control over."

Scott laughed.

"Enjoy your shoes," he said as he shut the door on his way out.

I could go into a lengthy description of extenuating circumstances they were dealing with at that time of their lives but I don't need to. You plug in whatever situations you are facing or use your imagination and the message is still the same. It has become the metaphor for this book.

Pick a pair of shoes that don't hurt your feet, and enjoy the journey Right Now!

Whatever the 'right now' has to offer you, find a way to enjoy it.

Does this book take a lighthearted look at hard stuff?

Absolutely!

Laughter has been proven medically to be an effective tool in treating everything from disease to depression. If we do not make you laugh maybe we will make you smile. If we do not make you smile at least you will have a few stories to take your mind off your troubles for maybe a minute or two.

"I am Janie Van Komen."

"And I am Lyn Austin."

Uniting our research, expertise, experience, and intuition we empower you with the survival tools of a happy traveler.

The purpose here is to find joy in 'your' journey. The disclaimer is we do acknowledge it is often challenging. We also know sometimes a good cry can relieve the anguish of the moment resulting in a kind of joy filled satisfaction. Joy is even found in the depths of a terrible trial when the moment of peaceful release at last fills your soul.

How do we know about all this stuff? We have been there. And more than likely we will be there again. But, in the meantime we want to share with you our most treasured tactics.

Come up out of the swampland of despair, self-pity, low self-esteem, and/or a self-centered focus. We are giving you a leg-up and showing you a different pathway to the top of Joy Mountain where the view is spectacular.

You are too tired, you say? You cannot get through the have-to-be-done's let alone take some silly hike up the side of a mountain?

They say a change is as good as a rest. We would love to describe the view from the top but it is not a matter of words. It is one of those things that enlivens every one of your senses and energizes your soul. You have to experience it for yourself. And trust us…. It is worth it! We will be with you every step of the way. You can do it. We believe in you.

And the first simple step of this journey is to clean out your shoe (or life) closet.

Did you know every time you open a messy closet it really does take energy out of your body? Go find one right now and open the door. Listen to the conversation that starts up inside your head. Everybody's closet has different stuff so the exact words might not be the same but probably the gist of the message rings true.

"These shiny black boots are way too big. They keep falling off the shelf, and Santa still has not invited me to go along on his midnight ride."

"Of course those blue heels are gorgeous, but the dress I wore them with the night I had to help those super heroes catch the bad guys got ruined when I fell into the tar pit. And nothing else matches this odd shade of blue."

"I would love to wear the little black pumps great Aunt Millie gave me, but the strap is almost broken. I cannot get rid of them. She might come over and ask to use the toilet. This is just an excuse so she can get into the back of my house, because she really wants to look into my closet to see if I still have the little black pumps she gave me (probably because the strap was almost broken)."

It is easy to pull out all the shoes, vacuum, dust, reorganize the stuff and put them all back. The hard part comes when you must choose which shoes to toss out, or give to the goodwill. And then which ones do you keep, especially when you are sentimentally attached to them for whatever reason.

DARE TO DUMP!

Union rules prevent Santa from ever letting you join his legendary Christmas Eve run. That color of blue will be impossible to match again. And if Aunt Millie is that sneaky who cares what she thinks.

The same thing is true for your life.

It is time to dump all the attitudes, guilt, inadequacies, and excuses that have cluttered and clogged up your life.

DARE TO DUMP!

This is where things get a bit tricky. The nature of the way our minds work, or in other words, the way we live with ourselves is called self-justification. We justify our motives and our actions first to ourselves and then to others.

For example: When you ate three pieces of cheesecake after dinner your brain knows this was a really bad health choice. It has to find a reason to make it okay... Rewind today's activities... The brain searches and selects reasons to justify...

"The mall was so crowded today you had to park your car a good half a mile away from the entrance, so you have walked at least a mile going to and from your car. You skipped breakfast, and you drank thirteen glasses of water."

If you add all those circumstances together it becomes acceptable that you dispatched way too much cheesecake. Then as an afterthought the brain gently suggests, "Just don't do it again." And you vow a solemn oath. "Tomorrow I am going to start doing healthy stuff." So now, with your tummy all satisfied and full of cheesecake, you are all right with yourself again.

Many body building or weight loss programs tell you before you start the course to better fitness, to go stand in front of the mirror naked and analyze your body. Today we want you to observe the person who lives inside of that body. Then you can start the course of finding immediate joy in your journey. It is sort of an inside fitness course.

Step outside the everyday skin you live in and evaluate every aspect of your life, no judgments, just honest observations. Act as though you are going to write a character analysis of this person called 'You.' Turn off the button on the radio frequency part of your brain that controls the inner critic. Today you must accept and believe. There is no good or bad in this exercise. It is only facts. You are just sorting, cleaning, and organizing the shoe closet of your life.

Lyn:

When you begin this process the most important aspect of what you are doing is to be honest with yourself. This takes great insight and courage. You will reveal yourself to yourself on paper. No one but you is going to read this. Seeing your flaws on paper is scary but crucial to your success.

"And the truth shall set you free".

We encourage you to be free of half-truths, or actual lies you have been telling yourself. When you take the time to see yourself, corns, bunions, and all, you will be much better equipped to begin to feel better about who you really are. After all, how can you fix something you cannot even admit is broken? Talk to yourself and put it on paper. You may feel confused while you take this internal inventory, as well you should be.

We are complex humans. We all have good and bad inside our deepest recesses. Let them out to breathe and dry. Once they are aired some of them will shrivel up and blow away. Your examination will show contradictions and that is okay too.

We guarantee if you take the time to do this self-inventory you will empower yourself. It is not as terrible as you might believe. Your true self already knows it all, so she will not be shocked with what you write down. Your closet is loaded with secrets and possibly a few skeletons shoved way back there like the pair of hot-pink stilettos you wore that one night in the city... Just seeing the heel of one of those dark secrets makes you shudder. You have no desire to go there. But coming from the queen of procrastination, I am here to tell you that sooner or later either you get it out in the open and rid yourself of it, or somehow, someway, it will surface when you least expect it, or are least prepared for it.

Mistakes, bad habits, past experiences whether good or bad can all be put away forever if you simply write them down. As you review the list tell yourself the lesson you learned. Put a check by it and then move on. Your mistakes should have equal respect as your talents and accomplishments. When you put them on an equal playing ground you will see that your awareness will indeed set you free.

This is your starting place. It is like those big maps in malls and road rest stops. They always have a distinguished mark designating 'You Are Here!'

To get where you want to go the first thing you have to know is where you are. This is where you are.

You Are Here!

Write your observations on a piece of paper or in a notebook. Date the page. When you are finished write these words:

I accept all of this. It is mine. I own all of it. This is who I am. I am so happy to know exactly where I am today. This is my starting place.

In observations of self...there is a difference between self-serving and selfless. 'Self-serving' is selfish and self centered, totally inwardly motivated and limited in purpose. While 'selfless' is taking into account one's own capabilities and moving them outward adopting endless possibilities.

Who you are is not one solid mass but rather bits and pieces of every person, experience, and sight you have ever encountered in this life.

Janie:

On my fiftieth birthday my husband and two daughters threw a surprise party for me. My husband told the girls to invite everybody who knew me. The thought was well appreciated. It was a surprise all right, a surprise for me and a surprise for all the people who came. The only thing any of them had in common was that they all knew me. Not only did they not know each other, they did not know anything about what I had done in my life with all those other people they did not know.

The party was a bit out of the ordinary. It was like my kids gathered up a bunch of strangers off the street and invited them over for cake and ice cream. Everybody was gracious, wished me a Happy Birthday, and left. My sister said it was the most unusual gathering of people she had ever seen all together in a non-public place.

For me the party was a life-changing event. It was the best gift my husband could have given me. When I walked into the explosion of surprise, each laughing shouting face retrieved a scene, a kind of movie clip from the memory bank of my life. This validated the reality of every different piece of myself. It was a mental big screen fifty-year-old epic movie experience of ME. Each person held a clip. And on this night they each came to splice his or her director's cut into the right place. The individual Oscar winning performances played out that night in my mind were far beyond Best Picture of the Year. The whole experience ranked right up there with Lifetime Achievement Award.

To look around that room and see what a multi-dimensional person fifty years of life whittled and carved me into was a spiritual experience. It was a unique moment to witness the fleeting illumination in each person's face of a memory or two. I was able to view my life as an observer looking in. This was the life flashing before your eyes experience without standing at death's door.

I highly recommend you reviewing the trappings of your own life and the people who have influenced it for both good and ill. It is a cathartic experience to realize all the different roles you have played. Look objectively at the people you have been, and the shoes you have worn. It doesn't matter how long you have lived. A person can be both Jekyll and Hyde in the same day. I bet if you count up the most shoes you have ever worn in one day you will be surprised how many pairs it is.

Just as a dirty messy closet zaps you with fatigue, a freshly cleaned and organized closet energizes your soul. Try it! Clean out a closet whether it be a shoe closet or something else that has haunted you for some time. Rip into it. Clean it with a vengeance and then step back and look at it... you will feel uplifted and rejuvenated. There is a sense of accomplishment and euphoria there. Pat yourself on the back and then prepare to move on to the secret closets of your life filled with cobwebs and junk that are zapping you out of a time of peace and fulfillment.

Once you have sorted the shoe closet, assessed which shoes to keep, the ones to give up to good will, and the ones to throw in the junk pile it is time to clean the mud off of the shoes you like to wear the most.

Question... If I shine up the shoes and make them look real spiffy, you know, the ones I like to wear the most, does that mean I have done it, and I will never have to clean muddy shoes ever again?

Chapter 2 - Clean the Mud off my Shoes…

Question? If I clean the mud off my shoes today I will never have to clean them again… Is that right?

Janie:

One day while de-junking my storage room I found a box containing some of my old journals. I noticed each January I set new goals.

January 1976 list included:

Totally clean the house

Lose weight

Be a better mom

Januarys 1977; 1978; 1979 and so on all had some version of the same goals as 1976.

Why did I commit myself to do the same goals year after year?

Did I fail to achieve my goal the previous year?

For a number of years I was an advisor to a women's group in our church. Many of the women were depressed from making lists of things they wanted to do. Each day they listed goals they wanted to accomplish. No matter how hard they tried, at the end of the day, they did not make it to the end of their goal list. For most of them tomorrow's list was already beyond reach. No matter how hard they worked, they never finished.

The secret is…. They will never finish.

We already know that secret, but if we admit defeat we feel like we have failed.

You have all heard the motivational speeches: "Writing down your goals is the first step to success." "Accomplish your goals and conquer the world."

The real secret is… You are never going to be finished… And that is Okay!

Many goals a person sets are never achieved because in fact they are not goals. What they are is actually a process, ongoing without end.

It is the journey not the destination. The process is a journey. A goal is an end point or rather a destination.

The only way a person can achieve the 'goal' of having all the housework done is if the entire family stands in the middle of the floor, naked and starving to death. As soon as somebody eats, gets dressed, or walks across the room there are more dirty dishes, soiled clothes, and crumbs on the floor. In other words there is more work to do.

As a matter of fact if you leave your house totally spotless, lock the doors, and go someplace else, the dust will still settle, the flies will still die on the counter, and the rain will still spot the windows.

Housework is not a goal it is a process. There is always something more to do, or redo. It will never be finished. When we look at housework as a goal we often become frustrated. No matter how hard we work, there will always be another thing to clean, organize, sort, or repair.

Nobody says: "Take this new car, fill it with gas, and you will never have to put gas in it ever again."

Or,

"I made breakfast for you kids yesterday, that should last you for the rest of your lives."

A process is ongoing without well-defined boundaries for beginnings and ends. A goal has well-defined boundaries, a definite start and an absolute end.

The reality is… the journey, or in other words, the process is what generates the most satisfaction. Process is work. Work is a gift. It relieves stress and gives a person purpose, fulfillment, and direction.

Achieving a goal is about ten minutes of glory, fame, or recognition, and generally there is a feeling of let down when it is over. When the Summer Olympics were in session it took between ten and twenty minutes from the announcement of the event's winners to when the athletes ascended the podium, received the placing of the medals, and listened to the National Anthem of the gold medalist. Winning any kind of medal in the Olympics is a huge accomplishment. Some of the winners of gold medals go on to great financial and popularity success. However, many of the silver, bronze, and even a few gold medal winners' fame is fleeting. Many of them, we, as a public, never hear of again.

Achieving goals must be kept in proper perspective. Goals are very important and will be addressed later in this book. The idea here is that achievement is extremely personal. We should do it for private reasons not for public recognition.

Janie:

Joanne Schlueter is probably one of the most successful baton twirling judge and coaches in the world. She only lived in my vicinity for a couple of years. I knew it was a privilege to take lessons from her. I was part of a team of four girls. Because of Joanne we began winning every team competition we entered. It was so much fun to win. It was such a high to walk into one of the competitions and hear a group of girls groan and say they did not stand a chance if we were there.

Then Joanne insisted I begin to enter the solo competitions as well.

As a part of the team I felt confident and invincible. On my own, in solo, I did not believe I could compete. When I balked about doing solo Joanne informed me that if I did not participate in the solo events I would be off the team.

The first solo event I entered I dropped my baton 13 times in a minute and forty-five seconds. Each drop docked my score by half a point. At the end of the routine I dropped the baton and accidentally kicked it with my foot. It rolled into the arena where others were competing. I was humiliated. I grabbed the darn thing, saluted, and marched out.

Joanne was waiting for me at the end of the aisle. I threw the baton at her feet and said, "See, I told you I couldn't do it."

Joanne scooped up my baton in one hand and grabbed me by the other. She pulled me underneath the partially extended bleachers of the gymnasium where the event was taking place.

"What do you think you were doing out there? Who were you twirling for? Who were you competing against? Do you think after judging 150 girls those judges are going to remember you? Do you think any of those girls in your division cared about anything except whether their scores were higher or lower than your score? You just don't get it do you?

"The only person you are competing against is yourself. The only thing you have to do is be a little bit better today than you were yesterday. And tomorrow will be easy because today you were lousy.

"You better figure this out real fast because if you don't, you are wasting my time and your parents' money. So either you decide you want to be the best you can be and do something about it or don't bother to cross my door again."

The next contest was a big one near Denver, Colorado. The second place trophy I won for solo competition was far more important to me than later when I won first place. I had believed in myself, worked for myself, and I knew this day's performance was equal to any other girl there. I learned the lesson. I got it. It was a turning point in my life.

That lesson stayed with me forever and I have applied it to every other thing I have ever tried.

The true and greatest satisfaction comes from the day-to-day conquests of the journey. If the journey was easy then achieving the goal does not hold the same exhilaration as if it was somehow difficult and challenging.

At the 2008 Summer Olympics, Gold Medal Gymnast Shawn Johnson was asked what went through her mind during the medal ceremony. She replied her thoughts went to all those days she wanted to quit or to give up and didn't. In other words during her recognition of the most glamorous and elaborate goal a gymnast can reach, her mind replayed the daily struggles which were the true joys of her journey. In that shining moment when all the world watched her standing on the podium with her scrubbed clean gold medal bigger than life smile, it was the 'process' of getting to the gold she focused on. It was the journey. The actual joy and glory of the goal was augmented by the sacrifices, trials, and efforts of the journey.

Every novelist knows it is the depths of despair, danger, and/or destruction of the protagonist that reaches out and grabs hold of its readers. It is the degree of suspense and personal trial the reader identifies with. In other words it is bringing the reader into the story alongside of the hero or heroine. The reader sees what the protagonist sees, feels what she feels, travels where she travels, and lives what she lives. This is what tethers the reader's heart and gives the reader kinship to the story. It keeps her returning and recommending the book again and again to others. Of course the climax or the 'goal' is important but it plays only a small part of a successful story. It is the journey or the 'process' the hero or heroine must endure and triumph over that makes the story enduring.

Janie:

When one of my children was asked to pray over the meal, he said, "Can we ask Heavenly Father to please bless all the food we ever eat so we don't have to pray anymore?"

Tasks in our lives that are repetitive are not goals they are process. Things happening in continual sequence are also considered process. Raising children is a continual sequential process.

Recently I heard a woman say, "I can't wait until my kids are eighteen years old, then I will finally be done with this mothering thing."

Looking at her comment from my perspective of eight married children, and one more who is an adult but not yet married, add to that a gaggle of grandkids, I smiled knowing the mothering thing never ends. It just changes. It is a process. There was no need to point it out to this woman. She will discover it for herself soon enough.

If frustration with your daily routine feels like you are spinning your wheels going nowhere, try sorting out the difference in your own life between the goals and the processes.

Janie:

When I started having babies I imposed a certain schedule of housework upon myself. My self-esteem was tied to whether I performed certain rituals of cleaning toilets, showers, vacuuming, dusting, and organizing specific things. I said to myself, "if I fail to do these things I am a failure as a wife and a mother."

As my babies arrived much faster than I originally planned, I realized I would drop dead from exhaustion if kept up the schedule I had set for myself.

In the beginning I collected and hand wrote meaningful quotes on tiny pieces of paper. I placed each one in the pocket of a freshly ironed shirt for my husband. This along with certain cleaning routines I considered to be essential duties. Each task had to be accomplished every week. In the space of five years I had four babies and replaced meaningful quotes with meaningful diaper changes and 2 a.m. feedings.

With each baby some of my goals had to be modified. At last I finally placed the vacuum cleaner in a direct line of vision from the front door and draped a dishtowel over the handle. That way if anybody rang the doorbell I would pick up the dishtowel as I opened the door. No matter how messy things were, it looked like I was in the middle of cleaning the house.

Once you discover what elements of your own life are process, you must then decide how much time you will devote to that process.

The next advice is crucial...

Give yourself permission to **STOP**.

For example: I will spend two hours cleaning the house today.

Give yourself the hardest, fastest, most efficient two hours you can muster and then stop. When you are finished and you put the vacuum cleaner away, do not start cleaning out the closet where you keep that vacuum cleaner. Leave whatever mess you have tagged as a must do into some other two-hour block. If you think you might forget about it... write yourself a note.

Plan what to do with your two-hour block of time and stick to the plan. Do not set the timer and then turn on your favorite television show. If you want to watch television, then watch it, but this is not your dedicated cleaning time. Do not split your attention with the internet, television, cell phone, or any other distraction. Stay focused.

When the time is up, stop. Reward yourself. Take a nap. Watch a favorite show. Read a book. Go shopping. Call a friend. Choose your own reward. Pat yourself on the back. You set a "goal" of two hours of work, you did it, and the "process" of keeping up your household will be better for it.

The argument that this goal versus process idea is a matter of semantics can be entertained, however, trust us on this. The way a person thinks about what she has to do has profound influence on how much she can accomplish. It also affects the energy a person generates in the performance.

Once you understand the difference between goal and process and incorporate this concept into the way you think, your daily routine, and your productivity will multiply. You will find time to do things you have been putting off, or that you have had a great desire to do but cannot seem to find the time.

Examine your life. Separate the processes from the goals.

Give yourself permission to be in control of the processes of your life. Give yourself permission to stop. If you do not do this there is a real possibility you will never find time to do what you landed on this planet to do. Your mission here will be found lacking. Uncontrolled processes can and will eat up your time and thus eat up your life. You must figure out how to manage them.

Once you give yourself permission to stop you will find you can also give yourself permission to do other things. Possibly there are things you avoided because you felt guilty doing 'them' instead of the 'necessary things.' This concept is discussed in greater depth in Chapter 7.

Another secret about process is there is no rule that says if it is 'your' process nobody else can play the game.

Janie:

As a newlywed it was a threat to me that my husband loved to cook. Some nights I made the meal and when he came home, he fixed something else to eat. Most of the time it was gourmet and exquisite. I would be furious. After all I spent hours trying to come up with some idea of what to make for dinner. In a few minutes with little thought, Robert fixed something delicious and better than my offering.

Then one day it hit me...I spent 'hours' trying to figure out what to fix. He spent 'minutes.' Robert loved to cook. It was his escape. He never had to think about it. It just came to him what to make. Why was

I spending so much time struggling when he loved food preparation? And why did I feel threatened because his food was better than mine? I started to adjust my daily routine. If I had some great idea for dinner, I fixed it. If I did not, I waited to see if he would. Sometimes I asked him if he would mind fixing dinner. This freed me to do lots of other things I preferred doing.

It was so liberating to let go of the idea he was trying to 'one-up' me. I quit thinking I was a bad cook, or worse, a bad wife. Instead of sulking I began praising him. I bragged about what he did to others. It was not long before he began trying to please me in other areas of our life as well.

Years went by and I found myself involved in a community project that was taking a lot of my time. We had a large family by now and I was counting on my husband to fix dinner every night, which was now a big job.

After about four weeks of this routine he had some stress at his work. He became resentful and angry about continually feeling pressured to fix the dinner.

"I think," he said to me with a rise in his voice, "that you look up and see what time it is and say to yourself, 'If I don't make dinner, Robert will come home and fix it.' So then you don't have to think about it anymore, because you know I will do it."

I paused a moment. I could see he was gearing up for a battle.

"Well, dear," I said, "there is no argument here. Yes, that is exactly what I do. I have been grateful that you are so willing to do that for us. If it has become a problem and you would rather not fix dinner, that's okay. I will try to rearrange my schedule in such a way that I can do it."

He was so surprised at my response that he just stood there for a minute or two and then said, "It's okay, I just wish you had asked me and not simply assumed I would do it."

My mistake was in not communicating with him. It was not that my role as the wife and mother dictated that I had to be the one fixing dinner. Meal preparation is a process. I apologized. I made an effort to be more vocal in my appreciation of his sacrifices, and life went on. The project ended, and I began to participate with him in the meal process again. Both of our self-esteems and egos were still in tact.

My mother-in-law was a little Dutch lady from Holland. She told me once that her hobby was cleaning the house. She set a goal of cleaning one room each day. That was her favorite part of the day.

The Dutch are the only people I know who will clean somebody else's house so they can afford to hire their own housekeeper. We had a Dutch Aunt who did this. When her own housekeeper came, my aunt cleaned right along side of the hired lady. This aunt would then fix a sit down lunch for the cleaning woman and herself. The two of them would sit, eat, share stories, and enjoy each other's company for about half an hour. Then the two of them would finish the work together.

If it's your goal to do three loads of laundry today because you love doing laundry, if doing laundry is where you gain your innermost feelings of purpose, fulfillment, and greatest satisfaction then by all means, have at it. But if laundry is merely another process of daily activities, then it's okay to instruct, allow, or permit others around you to do some of the laundry as well. Your self worth is not determined by how many towels you have folded this week.

It is not a threat to relinquish some of your process to others.

For mothers of younger children may I offer a word of advice? If you take your child to his or her room (or any other job you intend for them to do) and you stay with the child, you have the privilege to teach. Working alongside teaching the child exactly how to do the job and what is acceptable, creates a bond. The child will begin to understand what is the acceptable standard of completion for the particular job at hand.

However, if you *send* the child to do the job, the rules change. When he or she has completed the task, ask to see the work. If the child willingly and with pride shows you a job that you do not approve of or is not up to your standards, be very careful in your response.

When asked, a child usually will not want the job inspected if he or she does not believe it's up to standards set. If the child is anxious to show off the work, in my opinion (having raised 10 children, numerous neighbors, and a plethora of grandkids) accept the work. Praise the fact that the child completed the task. Make a mental note of the things you wish were different and next time or even later that same day, revisit the job *with* the child and show him or her how to correct the performance to a higher standard.

Never squash a child's self esteem. If they did a poor job, praise the effort they made. Be excited they did something, no matter how meager the offering. In most cases the reward will be a greater attempt on the child's part to better please you next time. It is the desire of most children to want to please their parents. They crave your attention and recognition.

Chapter 3 - If I buy Athletic Shoes...
Will I be an Athlete?

Being healthy is a state of mind plus effort, food, and movement. Nobody gets to choose the body she is born with, but she can choose what she will do with that body. The choice she makes affects every other aspect of her life.

We have all been given a place to reside. That place is called our body. It really is the only constant, and true home we will have until we die. We take it with us wherever we go.

Just as with the unwritten or unspoken house rules for an apartment, home, or dwelling place of where you sleep and keep your stuff, there are rules of coexistence with your body house as well.

For example:

What happens if you leave all the doors and windows open in your house and a terrible storm comes. The wind, rain, snow, sleet, or whatever the storm brings is bound to come inside. At the very least the temperature within the dwelling place will change.

The same holds true for your body house. You leave it unprotected and it will be defenseless from frostbite, or disease, or damage.

You did not get to choose your body. It came as part of the package deal of who you are. Being healthy is part state of mind, part effort, part food, part movement, and a part genetics and past history.

The 'You' that you are has to live your life with 'Yourself,' so the two of you must be nice to each other.

Recognize you are a dual being. You are the person who craves the whole pie, six chocolate chip cookies, and a hot fudge sundae complete with real whipped cream, nuts, and a cherry on top. You want this with no guilt, gained weight, fat grams, or sugar carbs. You are also the person who wants the toned abs, bikini body, healthy lifestyle, runs five miles a day, and drinks nothing but homemade juiced veggies and purified water.

You were given a body with moving parts. Why? So you can move, of course! The world around us is constantly moving. We should be moving right along with it.

You were not put here to be lumped into some dark room to stare continually at some dark box…. Oh, wait, that's called watching TV.

You were put here to move.

And here is the big secret about your body…

The more you move, the more you want to move. And the more you want to move, the better you feel. And the better you feel, the more your body rejects junk food and craves nutritious stuff. And the more nutritious stuff you eat, the healthier your body is. And the healthier your body is… the more you move.

And the more you move… the more you can accomplish. You can quickly make progress through the functional tasks you have before you and still have time for the fun stuff. Whatever it is you really want to do.

Some doctors are prescribing physical exercise to stave off depression, alleviate stress, as well as lose weight, tone up and strengthen weak muscles and limbs. It is also considered a necessary part of a healthy heart regimen. Exercise has been included in the fight against type 2 diabetes. Senior living centers that engage their members in physical activities find greater cognition, appetite, sleeping patterns, and general overall health.

Until recently in the western world doctors prescribed medicines for illnesses with little regard for the overall health picture of the patient. The Asian cultures have always incorporated the whole body wellness issue. As the world has become more globally minded the western world has begun to adopt the concept that all aspects of health and wellness are interrelated.

When you feel a tickle in your throat do you automatically assume that some virus has pegged you and there is nothing you can do but succumb to the disease?

You tend to believe your self-talk, because it is coming from a reliable source…yourself.

Who are the two selves that occupy your space?

If you are talking to yourself then who is the 'you' that is listening?

The physical self is useless without the other self, which is the spiritual or essence self of who you are. This reality is evident with death. Once the spirit or essence leaves the physical body, the physical body cannot sustain itself alone. There are numerous accounts of near death stories that validate the concept that there is a spiritual self that separates from the physical self at the point of death. It appears the spiritual self continues to exist without the body but the body cannot exist without the presence of the spiritual self. So for our mortal purposes of life as we know it in an optimum atmosphere we must be compatible with both of ourselves in an attitude of cooperation and enhancement.

Many people fool themselves into thinking they have no control over the physical self. They negate their ability to lose weight, stop smoking, or any other undesirable behavior as out of their control. They tell themselves that the addiction has them hooked and no matter what they do they cannot quit.

You have absolute control over your mind and your mind has absolute control over your body. You are what you believe you are.

Any kind of addiction comes from the physical self. It does not matter what kind of addiction it is. Smoking, drinking, drugs, sex, gambling, overeating, compulsive shopping, and every other addiction emanates from a desire to be physically satisfied and to feel those euphoric physical sensations. It is complicated. Whether or not there is some genetic tendency toward the addiction, the fact remains, if the person never smoked that first cigarette there would be no addiction to tobacco.

Cindi grew up with an alcoholic father. She reasoned if there was some kind of genetic link to alcoholism that if she began to drink alcohol it was very likely she too could become an alcoholic. She chose never to drink anything containing alcohol. She said, "I chose not to drink alcohol so I have never had to worry about becoming an alcoholic. I don't have to worry about my genes. I just chose not to go down that road."

Addictions, though physical in nature, rely on the mind as the psychological catalyst creating the desire to feel good in some way. This is where the body and the mind converge. The psyche craves the sensations generated by the physical body. Often the mind's imagined physical response is greater than the actual physical experience. The mind then desires the body to repeat the experience hoping for an equal or greater 'high' than in the previous episode. In cycles like this the reality is that senses are actually dulled with repeated exposure of the stimuli. The result then is the person must increase the behavior to achieve the same desired effect. This behavior escalates the addiction eventually to unrealistic proportions.

If you or someone you love is in a serious addiction cycle please seek professional help.

Another issue is if you find yourself using illness as an excuse for lackluster performance then you will find yourself suffering a myriad of health issues.

On the other hand there are many people, who are handicapped in one way or another with some kind of a health problem, yet they view themselves as healthy, and so they are healthy in spite of their physical limitations. Their quality of life is optimized in spite of their handicap.

Doreen was told that her cancer was terminal.

People around her commiserated saying, "Oh, it's terrible you are dying of cancer."

An angry Doreen responded again and again to this comment, "I am not dying of cancer. I am living with cancer."

This attitude bought her fifteen years of quality life after she had been told she may not last for the next six weeks, and would for sure be gone in three months at the most.

She was diligent in seeking medical help that would enhance the quality of her life in the most optimum way. She maintained a positive attitude. Yes, she had her days of crying and discouragement, but she chose not to linger in that mode and deliberately did things to make herself happy. Doreen constantly picked specific future events to work toward. Every day she was grateful to have this one more day. Finding joy in the journey became a game or a challenge to beat out discouragement. She watched many other cancer patients give up and allow the cancer to consume all joy. She could predict how long other cancer patients would live by their attitude.

Physicians are using visualizations to change attitudes concerning health issues. It has long been evident in the physicians' community that the person's attitude counts greatly in the overall recovery and health of the individual.

Physical movement of our bodies is essential to the overall well being of our minds and our bodies. The main problem with the concept of physical exercise is playing mind games. A person decides to get in better shape. The first day of exercise feels so good that usually the person goes way overboard. The second day the person then loses enthusiasm because of stiffness and lack of the same ability as the first day. Things usually go downhill from there.

Analyze your own physical activity in a day and a week. Review what you can do and how you can incorporate small baby steps as a way of life change.

There are three main paradigms for changing eating and exercise behaviors. The first is physical. The person wants to look good. This is the hardest paradigm because it fosters binge diets and temporary exercise programs. Once the goal is met the person returns to old habits.

The second paradigm is compliment or praise based. The person wants to be complimented on her appearance. She wants positive feedback from the people around her. This paradigm caters to the shock or amazement factor. Suddenly the person's appearance has changed. She has quickly dropped ten pounds and it shows. Many times it does not necessarily show in the actual body appearance but because the person feels better and things don't fit quite so tightly, she dresses more confidently or she buys new clothes. All of these invoke the surprise response of her personal community thus she gets the positive feedback she desires. The problem with this paradigm is that shock and amazement are short lived and so are the compliments. This paradigm also encourages quick fix diets, medical procedures, and exercises without a sustainable base.

Janie:

I met a woman who had some kind of a bypass surgical procedure. We were at a social gathering and she was telling me about how much weight she had lost. "Has it changed your life at all?" I asked her. "You bet," she answered. "Now I can eat all the junk I want as long as I do it in small amounts. It's my new lifestyle! I love the way I look and I did not have to give up a thing." I never saw her again, but I have wondered what eventually happened to her body if she did not change her lifestyle and never ate healthy food.

The third paradigm is a desire to feel better. The person changes her lifestyle so she will have more energy, health, or general well being. This is the most sustainable paradigm because it doesn't rely on outside forces as the reward system. The more the person does the better the person feels. It is not dependent upon the opinions or comments of someone else.

An amazing secret here is that almost any healthy established diet and exercise program will work. The reason there are genuine endorsements for any of them is that the success factor is mental. When the person decides to get healthy.... makes a true, honest, and unwavering commitment to a more healthy lifestyle, the method of getting there is not that important.

Diet and exercise binges to lose weight usually backfire. The person crashes into her programs and loses the weight. Once the weight is lost a reward is in order. A nice hot fudge sundae will suffice. Before long the original weight has been regained plus a couple more pounds just for good measure. Binge diets can also lead to anorexia and bulimia. If you find yourself locked into either or both of these cycles please seek professional help.

The only successful program is adopting a healthy lifestyle change: Eating smaller portions of healthy foods: Making your body move: And eliminating stress filled behaviors. (Note: There are many methods and reasons for body reduction. Please consult a physician if your overall health is threatened by a severe weight condition. There are many causes and problems associated with weight. This chapter only establishes that adopting a healthy lifestyle is paramount to maintaining a healthy regimen for life. It in no way suggests that this is the ultimate and only means for weight control or an oversimplification for being healthy. A personal health care professional is the only qualified person to make that kind of distinction.)

Sleep is another biggy. Recently a doctor treating a person with a sinus infection admonished the patient that she would not get well as long as she maintained a routine of sleep deprivation.

Lack of sleep can be just as dangerous a condition in driving a vehicle on the road as a drunk driver. Sleep is a very important part of a healthy life.

Be kind to yourself. Love the body you have. Exercise it. Nourish it wisely. Get enough sleep. Be grateful for what it can do. Do not dwell on what it is not and what it cannot do. Focus on what is and express gratitude daily for what you have.

If you follow this simple advice you will find it does not matter what kind of athletic shoes you buy. You will be as much of an athlete as you want to be.

Chapter 4 - What do You Think of My Shoes?

What do you think of my shoes?

Why are you asking the question? Are you looking for an opinion or an approval? If the answer you get differs from the answer you want then what? If you are looking for approval and you get a negative response how will that affect your self esteem?

Letting go of the opinions of others is much easier to talk about than it is to do. Many lives are swayed from day to day against the comments, opinions, and suggestions of well meaning or ill demeaning friends, family, and associates.

Lyn:

I allowed the opinion of others to nearly destroy my spirit more than once in my lifetime. At the age of ten years womanhood was thrust upon me when my period began and I had to wear a bra. By the fifth grade I was a C-cup. Some of the cruel boys in my elementary school started calling me Tits. By the 7th grade I developed a bad case of acne and the nickname turned to Tits and Zits.

I was 12 years old and I looked like the teacher instead of the student. The girls my age still looked like little girls and I was still a child in my heart, but my body was betraying me. Everyone around me expected and demanded I behave in a more mature manner. Many people young and old were simply disgusted by me and there was not a thing I could do about it. My 'I don't give a crap' attitude was only a sorry front. Often I cried well into the night.

My mother had been the tiniest tomboy in her class. She honestly had no clue of what I was going through. I don't blame her, but I will say that she simply could not understand because she had never been through anything like it. I instinctively knew that there was no sense in talking to her. I turned to my Dad's mother, Grandma Vera. I had inherited her genes. She had suffered the same ridicule and so she held a special place in her heart for me. She told me once that when she was a young girl she would bind her breasts with a flour sack to make her chest look flat. She loved me and knew what I was going through. I knew with her I could be myself without feeling self-conscious. Even now as she has passed on I still gain strength from her support and spirit.

I watched Grandma Vera struggle her whole life with her weight. She was never fat. She was a beautiful, classy, full-figured lady. Always impeccably groomed she had a purse and many times a hat, to match every outfit. She taught me, without saying a word, that you can look lovely even with extra weight. It was a matter of taking care of yourself. If you respect yourself, others will respect you. And if someone doesn't respect you because of your weight, they are not worth your respect.

Through my junior high and high school years many of the girls caught up to me in height and weight. Many had their own sad case of acne. Mine went away. But no one ever caught up to me in the boob department. Twiggy was the teen icon in my day, so big boobs were not as acceptable as they are now. People thought I was "easy" because big boobs made you look slutty. Even though I was raised in a strict moral religion and was a virgin on my wedding day, I was considered wild. Girls were jealous, parents were disgusted (at least the mothers), and boys oogled.

Whispers were common when I walked into the room and the wild rumors raged. Even though I knew none of these things were true, no one else, not even my friends, teachers, and parents were quite sure.

The result of all of this negativity put my self-esteem lower than an ant farm.

I did have talent though. It was my saving grace. I could sing and dance and act. Looking back now I wonder how I dared do any of it. I can't even count the times I was told, "You have such a pretty face, if only you could lose 10, or 20, then 50 pounds." I felt fat since the fourth grade and almost everyone I knew reinforced my belief. Hurtful names like Two-Ton-Tessie (I was 5"4 and weighed 125lbs), and Lynnard with plenty of innards, (5"4 and 130 pounds). The worst part of this whole mess is I believed those jerks. And the negative thoughts consumed me. I carried this low self-image with me throughout the first 40 years of my life.

During my softball playing years, I tore my Achilles' tendon. It hadn't healed properly and gave me great pain every time I tried to exercise. With the inactivity I began gaining even more weight and in nine years I added another eighty pounds to my 230. In January of 1991 I tipped the scales at 310 pounds. I found a new doctor that gave me hope for my tendon problems and I had surgery to correct it. I knew it would only be a few weeks before I would no longer have any excuse for not exercising.

It was time to do something, but my addictive negative self-talk told me I would never succeed. While I was off work recuperating from the surgery I decided to start changing my internal dialog. But before I could do that I was curious to see if my pessimism was really as bad as I thought. I took out a notebook and wrote Negative and Positive across the paper and divided the page into two columns. I would consciously review what I was thinking to myself and mark a check for every positive or negative thought during this one day. I still remember my first thought that morning was," what should I fix for breakfast?" Answer--cereal. "You don't have time for anything else," I said to myself, "because you slept too late. You slept too late because you are fat and that makes you tired. Cereal is the worst thing to feed your kids. They are going to grow up and be fat like you, and it is going to be all your fault!" (5 negatives in the first thought of the day.) Next, deciding what to wear... l will leave that one to your imagination. I will tell you it had 22 negatives in it before I was dressed and I wasn't even going anywhere important that day! At the end of the day I kept the record of my self-talk, I had given myself 4 compliments and 742 destructive, negative thoughts about myself.

I racked up a bundle of them just sitting at home recuperating. When I was out in public it was several times worse than at home. Every time I walked by a mirror I would be shocked and disgusted with my image and I wondered why my own family would go anywhere with me and why my husband stayed. The simplest tasks were agony. For years I never entered the grocery store without thinking that every person in the store was disgusted with me for needing to buy food. I never walked across a parking lot or through a crosswalk when I didn't imagine the people in their cars laughing and making jokes about me denting their cars if they hit me.

Now I might have been fat, but I was not stupid. I had read enough self-help books to know my negative thoughts were actually making me heavier. I pondered this concept all that afternoon. It finally came to me. The realization that my thoughts had helped me to get to this terrible state hit me hard. The next idea manifested... if my brain was that powerful, then all I had to do was be in charge of my brain and things could begin to change. The question was how to do it?

I started thinking of all of the things people had said about me that had added to my own self-destructive dialog. I decided to make a list of the people who had hurt me with their cruel and thoughtless remarks. Although there were several names on the page, I was surprised that the actual list wasn't near as long as I thought it should be. Some of the names on that list were boys I could hardly even remember and I had not seen for 20 years.

I had let a handful of people destroy my self-image and I am sure the thought of me never even crossed their minds! The other people on the list were a little harder to take. These were people that were still in my life and whom I loved very much. And amazingly enough, I knew they loved me.

My grandfather, whom I always loved and looked up to, made a careless remark that nearly killed me. He was watching my ten-year old little sister eat a homemade cookie my grandma had just taken out of the oven. When she finished it she reached for another. My grandpa looked over at me with a disgusted sneer and then back to my little sister and said, "What are you trying to do, end up looking like your sister?"

This insensitive and cruel remark did no one any good. My grandma, who loved me unconditionally and would cut off a limb before purposely hurting anyone, was appalled by his comment. Grandpa went to his grave without apologizing to any of us. And you know what? We still all adore him.

The great thing about living a life with a family is that you have millions of opportunities to fill other people's shoeboxes with good memories. And then when someone hurts your feelings you have plenty of good memories to fall back on. One hurt doesn't empty the box. And if you are still breathing after you get hurt, the incident did not kill you. So my suggestion to you is to put the comment or incident into the box of stuff going to the garbage dump and get rid of it.

Oftentimes when those we love the most are trying to be 'helpful' in some kind of frustrating circumstance, turning to an outsider that is able to give you the lift you need in spite of whatever the problem is can possibly be a life saver.

True girlfriends are a priceless commodity because nine tines out of ten they have been through what you are going through right now. And the way they got through it may not be the way you choose, but at least they have empathy for where you are and sometimes just talking about it can ease the pain.

And while we are talking about friends, don't forget God and your angels. They are always one call away--their lines are never busy, they always pick up when they see it is you on the caller I.D. and they have no off-limit hours, But remember, you do have to <u>ask</u> for their help. So talk to them and ask them to bring you healthy friendships, the kind where you both gain happiness and peace from the connection. God and the angels are ready and wanting to help with whatever you need in your life. Take advantage of this God-given right and privilege.

Lyn:

Okay, back to my list. I now have this list of people in front of me who had hurt me in some way throughout my life. It took courage but finally I added one more very important name, perhaps the most important name...my own.

I looked over the list and with the exception of one boy from high school, I didn't want any of them dead... So what should I do with this list now? To this day I don't know what made me decide to do this but it was very effective. I hobbled on my crutches outside on that freezing January day and I lit the paper on fire. I dropped it in the snow and I watched it slowly shrivel up and burn to ashes. Every ash had blown away before I realized that I had been holding my breath. I let out a slow deep breath, filled my lungs with fresh frigid air and said out loud, "Good bye, to all of you who knowingly or unknowingly have hurt me. I forgive you and you now have no power over me anymore."

Instantly I felt better. Again I had a strong desire to make another list. I would keep this one. I opened a beautiful new journal and wrote on page 1, People who have loved me throughout my life. This list astounded me. It was 5 times as long as the negative one. And of those who made both lists I could now see so many good things they had said and done for me over the years.

I thanked God for the many people in my life who loved me. I asked for His help in making the proper decisions to get me on the road to recovery. I knew that diet and exercise were not going to be enough for my particular case. Throughout these years of constantly gaining weight I had tried at least a dozen different diets. I was 36 years old and I felt 70. I knew without a doubt if I did not get some weight off and soon I would not be alive to raise my children. I had seriously investigated a gastric by-pass. I was scared and confused. I read every article I could find about it. I talked to anyone I knew that'd had the surgery. I now pleaded with God and my angels to give me the courage to make a decision and stick to it.

After my heart-felt prayers I was resting on the couch in my living room in front of a cozy fire, writing in my journal. I needed to sort my thoughts of the turbulent day. It was time for the kids to be getting home from school. Out of the window I watched the group of neighbor children walk toward our home after getting off the bus. My daughter, Kerilyn, was 9 years old. I noticed her stop as she listened to something a little girl that lived further down our country road was saying. And then without hesitation, I watched as Kerilyn pushed the other girl in the chest hard enough to knock her on her butt into a snowdrift!

I couldn't believe what I had just witnessed! My daughter wouldn't hit someone especially smaller than her unless she had a really good reason. Don't get me wrong, my little and only girl had 3 older brothers. They would all protect her with their lives, but they also used her quite regularly for their guinea pig. They tried all sorts of wild games and inventions with her as the fall guy. She had learned to protect herself more than once. This solitary incident was, however, out of character for her.

"*Kerilyn, why did you hit that girl? I asked.*

"*She said something that made me mad."*

"*What did she say?"*

Silence...

Kerilyn tore her backpack from her shoulder, dropped it next to the piano and walked into her bedroom shutting the door behind her.

I pulled my crutches to me and hobbled to her door, knocked lightly, and then went in. She had one tear rolling down a porcelain cheek. Her deep, rich brown eyes, so much like her father's, pled silently with me not to ask the question again. Because I was so in-tune with my angels on that day, I knew what the other girl said had something to do with me.

I sat down heavily on the edge of her bed, and lightly touched her shoulder, "Kerilyn, you know you can tell me anything. What did she say?"

With an angry sweep of the back of her hand, she rubbed the tear off her face and ducked her head. I could see I had not made the part separating her braids exactly straight on the crown of her head that morning.

I waited.

She took two deep breaths and then she whispered. "She said that someday I would grow up to be as fat as my mom."

The next day I scheduled my by-pass surgery.

Take the attitude of listen, file, and forget. Evaluate the important messages. You then have to choose if you want to do something about them. Don't be swayed by other's ideas of what you should or should not be. You choose. Discard the riff raff. Nobody is living your life except you. No matter what, always choose your own pair of shoes.

There is a Dutch saying: Do what you want, because no matter what you choose to do the hens will still cackle.

 In other words you can't please everybody.

The most important person to please is yourself. This isn't about being selfish. This is about having your own house in order before you can effectively help somebody else.

Janie:

It was my maiden voyage into adulthood. A week following our high school graduation three of us moved to the 'big city' into an apartment to attend college for summer semester. It was a metropolis with upscale retail stores not far from where we lived.

A girl in the adjoining apartment invited all three of us to visit her aunt's place of work. This aunt was the curator of all the designer clothing for the most expensive private showing room of the premier retail business in this city. She offered to let us come one day when the showroom was closed and try on any private label clothing item we wished. She thought it would be fun for us to see up close what true designer duds were like. There were six of us in all who traipsed up to the store that day.

Phrases like, 'A once in a lifetime opportunity,' floated back and forth between us as we walked to the location at the specified time.

After a brief lecture by the aunt of the rules governing this adventure, all the girls began swishing the hangers back and forth on the rods looking for just the right fit or style.

All of the girls except me, I just watched with amazement. I could not believe we were really seeing designer clothing in person. I was curious to see what each girl picked out. However, I made no attempt to choose anything for myself. I wasn't even aware that I was not part of the frenzy.

One girl grabbed my sleeve and pulled me into the rack attack. "Come on," she said, pushing me almost off balance into the swaying wall of expensive couture, "which one do you like?"

It was a simple question. It should have been a simple answer.

"Uhhhh," I said as I stepped off the hem of a long drapey skirt now dusting the hardwood floor. "Uhhhh," I repeated adjusting the skirt properly back onto its hanger.

With this exchange several girls suddenly noticed I hadn't really joined the activity. "What's the matter?" another girl asked. "Just pick something. What do you like?"

I gingerly pushed at the dress in front of me like it had a disease. "Oh, my mother would hate that one." I said. Then holding the arm of something straight out from where it was hanging, I smiled, "Actually, I think my mother would choose something like this."

"Your mother? Your mother? Nobody cares about what your mother thinks. This is all pretend. None of us can afford any of this stuff. Your mother isn't even here. What does your mother have to do with any of this?

"The question is what do you like?" said one girl with a distinct emphasis on the word "you."

It was my first real panic attack, and it was a turning point in my life. In that nano second of eternity, time froze for me. It was just like it is on the big screen when some corny actor has to catch up with what the audience already knows. I had based all my opinions and life choices up to that point on what I perceived my mother wanted me to choose. I suppose that not unlike most children I desired her approval of me. In my case however, it was so much so, that I had no idea what my own opinions were.

My eyes went blurry and I feared I might faint as my heart raced and the perspiration beaded on the sides of my head. I blinked not being able to clearly see anything, and I grabbed the first outfit I could reach. It was a one-shouldered sling looking thing and I stated with resolve, "This is the one I like the best."

All of the girls stared at it and then at me. I was a conservative, not thin, sensible shoes kind of a gal and this was a plunging neck, revealing, swanky deal. To wear it a person needed the kind of figure that could only be airbrushed on magazine spreads.

"Well," I said, "You said it was all pretend anyway, so if I were in some other kind of life, this is the one I'd like the best."

"Okay," one of the girls shrugged, and they all went back to their own choices.

I was trembling with adrenaline exhaustion over the personal revelation no one seemed aware of except myself. I marveled at the blankness of my mind. I had no idea what my own opinions and/or choices were. I only knew what I perceived my mother wanted me to choose.

I say, perceived, because in later years I learned that I was wrong about my mother's ideas. I was looking at them through the experience and observations of an eighteen year old. Teenage observations are mostly like the house of mirrors at the amusement park. Although you see the image clearly, it is always in some way distorted. These observations cannot be compared to the wiser desires of a mother with quite a few more life years and experience under her wings.

Our opinions, conclusions, and even our observations are based upon our age and life experiences. A tiny child might reach out to touch a hot stove because the red color of the burner looks pretty. An older person has the experience and knowledge that the red color means it is too hot to touch and the resulting burn would be painful.

A major mistake many people make is the assumption family members or others living and/or working together are all having the same experiences.

For example: The Dad comes home from work. Johnny asks Dad, "Can we go to McDonald's for dinner?"

Dad says, "No, we can't afford to eat out all the time," and then Dad goes into his bedroom.

Mother immediately assumes something bad has happened with Dad's work. Maybe he isn't going to get his bonus. Maybe he got fired. Maybe he got a cut in pay.

Johnny thinks, "Dad never wants to do what I want to do."

Dad responded to Johnny's request in that manner because he had a terrible headache. He wanted to stay home. It was easier to take the money route than have to explain his real reason for not going to McDonald's.

All three people were in the same room. All three people heard the same conversation. Each person then processed that information into a different conclusion according to his or her age, experience, and perception.

We must be cautious in judgment of others. We must also be very cautious about accepting someone else's judgment of us.

The best rule of thumb is… ***Choose your own pair of shoes and allow others the same privilege.***

Chapter 5 - Wearing Slippers to Shop is Tacky

Stop judging the whole world against your perceptions.

Janie:

For twelve years after I married we lived in a 'high rent' district. I had no idea I was being indoctrinated with the mores of the area until I moved into a lower income level community. In our high rent location I always 'dressed' to go shopping at the grocery store. In the new area I noticed that women wore curlers in their hair, sloppy clothes, and heaven forbid, slippers. I saw every kind of slipper from simple flip-flops to big obnoxious fuzzy things that looked like floor dusters.

I maintained my decorum. Certainly I was above their standards. I would not be caught dead entering the grocery store looking like they did. That is not until the week after my sixteen-year-old daughter was killed. I forced myself to go through the motions of necessity. One morning when we were out of milk. I took my older kids to school and then stopped at the grocery story to pick up milk and a few other things on my way home.

I grabbed the gallon of milk and the other items and hustled to the checkout. I had to hurry in order to get the other kids to the elementary school on time. As I stood in line waiting for the lady ahead of me I stared down at the floor hoping nobody spoke to me. I had no energy for conversation. I was barely functioning. Staring at the feet directly below me on the floor I had a strange sense that they belonged to somebody else. Hmmm, somebody else had slippers just like mine. Actually I think those are my slippers I thought. The right one has the stain from me dropping grape juice on it. Who is wearing my slippers in the grocery store I mused?

I checked out and those slippers followed me out to the car. At last I registered as I climbed into my car, they were my feet. I had worn slippers to shop and I didn't care.

Time passed. That pounding aching pain in my chest subsided. My thinking cleared up. I reflected on the day I wasn't sure whose feet were beneath me; let alone what they were wearing. On that day I dropped all my biases about what people wear to grocery stores.

I try really hard not to be prejudiced about other people and their circumstances, but darn it, those thoughts just jump right into my head as the first responder to the automatic assessment of what my eyes see.

Changing Perceptions. Again… Stop judging the whole world against your perceptions. It becomes exhausting to mentally keep track of biases, criticisms, and opinions. It is so much easier to cheer for the underdog in the movie theater watching that poor unfortunate person or family on the big screen than it is in your day-to-day life. Choose your own value system, but be open to being one with the universe and all the good things in it. Human nature dictates the lie that it is somehow satisfying to focus on all the imperfections, dirt, and garbage there is in the world. Depression is vogue.

Happiness, however, comes from recycling the garbage, cultivating the dirt, overlooking imperfections, seeing value, and loving others into a desire to be better.

Janie:

Back before computerized checkout machines scanned the sale items, calculated prices, noted quantities, discounts, inventory, and taxes, back when I was young and stupid, there was a chain discount store that I made fun of to anybody who would give me audience.

"They send their employees to a special school," I would say with an air of superiority. "The object is to teach them how to be the most incompetent sales clerks ever to work in a store."

I made a point of sighing loudly and rolling my eyes as I watched the clerk pull the tags from the purchase items and then match the tag to a particular slot to drop it into. I acted out all the irritated body language, from the exaggerated watch checking, to tapping my pen loudly next to my checkbook. If the sales person had to call for any kind of help I'd say, "Oh brother," and/or "Not again."

One day of exasperated purchasing from the most incompetent clerk I had ever seen in this or any store, I was noisily gathering up my bags at the end of the counter with all the righteous indignation I could muster.

The lady behind me stepped forward and said to the clerk, "I am so sorry about your mother. I can't believe you are here at work." Then she put her arms around the young woman and gave her a hug.

I have no idea what the problem was. I only know how ashamed I was of my critical behavior and attitude. I said a silent prayer for the woman and her mother as I left the store. I also prayed for my own repentant soul.

Since that day whenever I see a person who appears to be behaving in a fashion that before I would have criticized whether it be clerking, stocking shelves, managing, or any one of a dozen other public positions of service, I send them love.

I say, "Whatever makes you behave this way, I send you all the love you need, to change, work it out, improve, or be comforted. Whatever is your problem, I send you love."

In the folklore of almost every culture is found some version of this concept: You get what you give. Or what goes around comes around.

People are changed when they feel safe. They feel safe when they are loved.

Unconditional love is exactly that. Love without conditions. This doesn't mean condoning behavior that goes contrary to your core beliefs. Remember it is the behavior you do not accept not the person.

Janie:

With ten children I had about every different kind of teenage behavior including the good, the bad, and the ugly. I told my kids." If you get with friends who are doing things you don't want to do, call me. Even if you have done something you shouldn't do, call me. I will come and get you, no questions asked. I won't lecture you. I will just see that you get home safely.

Now, you have to know... Tomorrow I may have a few words of advice, criticism, reprimand, or punishment, but tonight I just want you to know that I love you and want more than anything for you to be safe."

Most of the time when you think you are angry with someone for behavior you don't approve of, it is not anger you are feeling it is either disappointment or fear. Try to evaluate what you are truly feeling in this kind of situation. When you can express your true feelings the impact is much greater.

If you say, "I am angry," immediately the other person becomes defensive. It is human nature to defend yourself even if you know you are wrong or you know you made a mistake. If you can take the anger out of it and explain why you are disappointed or what you fear, the other person has a much harder time justifying his or her behavior.

"Susie, you are such a good kid. I have always felt like I could trust your judgment. I want to believe you are safe. What you did was so disappointing to me. I am brokenhearted that now you will have to prove to me I can depend on you again. I need to be able to trust you to make right choices. I am afraid of what could happen to you if you do this again, or make a habit of what you have done."

Janie:

One day my daughter had a couple of friends over to play. After a little while one girl said, "Why don't we call, so and so, and see if she can come over and play with us?"

The other little girl said, "Don't you remember we don't like her right now because she played with Brittany yesterday at recess instead of us."

"Oh yeah," said the first girl, "I forgot. It makes me tired sometimes trying to remember who we like and who we don't. It's so hard because it changes all the time."

At first when I heard this conversation I had to stifle my laughter. Upon a second consideration I realized this is one of the major problems with the whole world. We have to keep track of who we like and who we don't. This is exhausting and hard to remember. Is it the American Indians, the Germans, the Jews, the Japanese, the Bosnians, the Vietnamese, the Iranians, or the Iraqi's? Oh wait, I think it is my next door neighbor with the barking dog. Who is you don't like this week?

Many times we compose our own ideas of what another person thinks about us and gear our actions to what we think they expect. Usually it is without merit or base. Then when we don't get the desired response from that person we were trying to impress or make happy, we are offended.

Why can't we as women of the world, the nurturers, the compassionate ones, why can't we simply send love to all people. It will make others suspicious at first. But in time if we are sincere and do not give up, others will have to believe us. Maybe it will be contagious like a plague. A plague of love, of goodness, filling up the whole world, suffocating hate, envy, killing, and destruction.

Maybe as the women of the world we can create an epidemic of Peace!

Chapter 6 - Get Out of the Shoebox

The Shoebox of life is safe. Stepping out of your comfort zone is the only way to confront and overcome your fear.

Janie:

I grew up in a small town with all the small town idiosyncrasies. Nobody went anywhere unless it was out to the 'dry farm' to work. The local newspaper printed a big write up if anybody took a trip farther than 100 miles away.

When I was in first grade my friend Barbara and her family were transferred with the military to live in the Azores. I thought that was the most exotic thing I had ever heard of.

My Dad was a farmer with animals. We hardly ever took a vacation. Who would take care of the animals? All I could think of was how lucky my friend was to be able to live someplace far away. I could not even find The Azores on the map. This made it even more exotic and enticing to me.

As soon as possible I began learning a foreign language. I studied Spanish. I wanted to be fluent so I worked very hard to make the proper sounds and accents. Someday I would go to foreign countries. I wanted my Dad to be in the military so we could go to strange and wonderful places like The Azores. I dreamed about marrying somebody from another land.

I did not care where I went as long as it was out of town... way out of town.

Be careful what you wish for.

I married a man from The Netherlands. Although it was romantic, my life was not all exotic. And it definitely was challenging to mix cultures on a daily basis. However, I have never been sorry I made this choice.

Until my marriage, in the scope of my limited vision, I thought taking one major foreign trip, perhaps a tour of Europe, would be the most exciting once in a lifetime thing I would ever do. After my marriage I was stunned in the discovery of the matter of fact way my husband thought nothing of continent hopping. He had family on both sides of the ocean. He watched tickets to Europe like most people watch the stock market. When the price drops.... you buy!

I visited The Netherlands about 15 times and then we lived there for two years. I have also been to England, France, Belgium, Germany, Italy, Canada, Morocco, and Mexico. I think I have seen thirty-five of our fifty States. It has been exciting, educational, fulfilling, and 'exotic' traveling and experiencing all kinds of things in these many locations

You would think my wildest dreams have come true. The secret truth is... traveling away from home scares me to death.

For some strange reason things happen when I leave home. Here are a few of the major things. (The list of not so tragic occurrences is too long to mention here.)

My Grandma Wood died suddenly of a ruptured bowel

My maternal grandmother (who was my second mother) died. (I'd been very close to both of these women and neither was 'that old' when they passed away.)

My husband's Father had a major heart incident and appeared at death's door.

Three neighbors died.

My nephew died.

9-11 happened

Twenty-five years after the original heart incident Robert's Dad died abruptly while we were in Europe.

My parents were in a head-on auto collision. My mother sustained a broken neck among 13 other broken bones and very serious internal injuries.

And then ten years later while my husband and I were in Disneyland my mother died of congestive heart failure

I have questioned whether I should ever go anyplace. I have to ask myself, "What would have happened differently if I had stayed home?"

The Shoebox of life is safe, comfortable, and controllable. It can also be confining, blinding, stifling, and deceptive.

In the comforts of life we often develop complacency. Our growth is stunted. The reality is that all of those tragedies of mine would have occurred in my life whether I had been home or not. It is a false concept that a person can better control the elements of his or her life from the comforts of home. Don't get me wrong, I am not suggesting to run off with reckless abandon to one's responsibilities. I am saying the fact remains… life happens.

Retreating to the safety and renewing of the shoebox is acceptable for fortification, but creative living, solutions to problems, and adventures are found only when we step out of the known into the unknown. Moving from the known into the unknown is one of the greatest fears of life.

Many women will remain with abusive, alcoholic, or some other disgusting version of a man rather than face the fear of an unknown life without those problems.

What is in your shoebox? What is in your comfort zone? What are your fears? How do you cope with them? What are you doing to face 'the outside' world of your life?

It is not all about travel or actually going away. Maybe you have a gift, talent, or desire you have always wanted to pursue. Fear of failure paralyzes the progress of individuals, of families, of society.

One woman said she continued to attend school. If she did not graduate she could count on two things. First, her self worth was constantly reinforced when she received good marks or an 'A' grade. And second, as long as she was in school she would not fail in the real world. School is structured and defined, life is not.

This chapter is not about the influence of others. That topic is covered in chapter 4. This chapter is looking at what is your excuse to yourself. Nobody else is involved in this discussion. This is you finding the courage to evaluate where you live inside of your 'you-house' and decide how you can step outside of the non-growth places where maybe you have become stagnated, where your flower garden needs to be moved to a place with greater sun. Perhaps you never step outside to see your flower garden and you are in reality retrogressing in your progress.

Unfortunately we do not get a dress rehearsal for this life. This is it. It is all improvisation. We make it up as we go. Do not get to the end and wish you'd had the courage to step outside the shoebox of your comfort zone to experience life to its fullest.

Take baby steps. Try one thing. If it works, congratulations… keep working on it, if it does not try something else. Open the door of your shoebox and step outside even if all you do is take a deep breathe and close the door again. At least you opened the door.

Lyn:

I had the privilege of spending some time in Mississippi while my husband worked there. This was my first time living in that part of the United States.

I have always considered myself unbiased. When I was growing up my father taught auto mechanics at Job Corp in Utah. He taught me all people are created equal in God's sight and therefore it should be the same way in mine. We often invited different races and cultures to our home for Thanksgiving and other holidays. However, outside of a roommate in college from Taiwan and Hispanic friends in Idaho, at that time I'd had very little interaction with other ethnicities.

In Mississippi where I lived I was the minority. Not only did I look and dress differently, but when I spoke, people stared at me. It was a little frightening for me at first. I was definitely stepping outside my previously all white shoebox. Although I was the different one, I had never met a friendlier, kinder, and helpful group of people in my life. They treated me with respect even if I was the odd duck with the funny accent.

I was impressed with the politeness and respect the Mississippians showed to others, especially their elders. I witnessed a woman shopping with her grandmother and her young daughter. It was so refreshing to hear, "Yes Ma'am" and other kind words as the three generations conversed.

Also, it became evident to me that we as women are more alike than we are different. One day I had the dreaded chore of going to the Laundromat. There were five African American women and myself there. It was evident to me that the five of them were all acquainted. I felt out of place and a little lonely. I put my clothes in the washing machines and sat down to read.

The rest of the ladies were passing a piece of paper around the group. Each one looked it over very carefully, marked something on it, and then discussed it with the next person as it was passed on. My curiosity was killing me, so I finally walked over and asked one of them what they were reading. All the ladies were friendly to the weird, nosy, white lady with the funny accent. They explained the paper was a word search of names in the bible. Then they asked me if I would like to help them figure out the puzzle. We enjoyed working on it together. Soon our conversation transferred over to other interests, such as children and grandchildren and life in other parts of the country. Someone mentioned cancer and my face must have blanched because one of the ladies asked me if I was all right. I told her my brother had cancer and I was very concerned about him. One of the dear women explained her son was a minister. She had me write down my brother's name so her congregation could pray for him.

I left there that day feeling better about my brother and less homesick so far away from home.

All of this happened because I was willing to step out of the comforts of my little shoebox of life for one minute and talk to others.

I don't care what the naysayers say. I believe the majority of people are all striving for similar things in this world--love for self, family, and country, financial security, spiritual knowledge, and peace. I also believe that because women are the more compassionate sex, we must take the lead, step out of our shoeboxes, and reach out to others.

Evaluate where you stand in the friendship category. Are you willing to step out of your shoebox to be a friend or help someone in need? Do you ever look around to see if somebody is in need?

Lyn:

The concept of not having friends is something I have had little experience with, but I had a serious conversation with a lady recently that revealed to me that she has never had a good friend--a friend in the true sense of the word-- girlfriends to be exact--the kind that you can pour out your heart to. The kind of friend that you can say anything to and she won't flinch or bring it up to you later or hold it against you.

There have been a billion things written about friendship and girlfriends, but after this conversation, I realized how painful it must be to see those books on the shelves or that poster of the little girls on the fence with their arms wrapped around each other when you do not have a friend. It made me stop and think about what that might feel like and the images scared me.

I have lived through some very tough times and my true friends and family were the only thing that kept me alive. Some of my best friends have been men. My late husband Kerry was my best friend for over thirty years, even during a time when we separated. Now my best friend is my husband, Butch. I would rather be with him than any person in the world.

Janie has told me many times that she feels the same way about her husband, Robert. When you are looking for new friends, please do not limit your choices to a certain type of person, race, religion, or sexual orientation. You may learn lessons from your new friend that you never dreamed of and they will learn from you. No matter who you are you have qualities to admire and ideas to share.

Now that we have covered alternative friendships, and since this is a girly kind of book, we would like to discuss woman-to-woman friendships and how to have positive ones.

Lyn:

Years ago my sister-in-law, Wendy had to move away from our hometown to Butte, Montana for her husband's work. Wendy had many friends in the area where she grew up, but she was still nervous about moving to an unfamiliar area where she knew no one. She had a new baby and so she did not plan on working outside of her home for a while. What would she do with her day and how would she fill her time. As she voiced her concerns with me I said, "Wendy, just take your personality and get out there. Go to church, join a civic club, take a class in a hobby you enjoy. Visit with the bank teller, the grocery store clerk, the florist and you will begin to make friends.

A year later we visited Wendy and her family in Montana. She was happy, busy with her life and had many new friends. I asked her how all of this had happened so quickly. I will never forget what she told me, "I learned that in order to have a friend you must be a friend. I sat in this little apartment for a while in my self-pity and I realized that I was never going to find friends if I did not step out of my living room and start talking to people. When I started doing that it became easier and easier." When Wendy moved from Butte, she left many friends, some of which are still in contact with her years later.

Now, granted, Wendy has a bubbly personality and I am sure many of you may be thinking; but I am shy and I am afraid of rejection, and I have been like this my own life and it is too late to change.

Remember that old adage is still true, "In order to have a friend, you must be a friend." Can you bake a cake? Can you take that cake to someone you heard has been hurt in an accident and has a broken leg? Now, instead of just dropping it at the door and rushing away, could you sit down and visit with the person for a few minutes? Could you offer to pick up a few things at the store for her? While you are visiting you notice that she likes to do crossword puzzles, so do you. The next day when you bring her the groceries, you bring along your latest puzzle with three words you can't figure out. She knows the answer to one of them right away because she has seen the movie ten times. She can't believe you have not seen it. Perhaps you could stay for dinner and the two of you could watch it together. You cook spaghetti while she hobbles on crutches setting up the movie.

A friendship is kindled.

Lyn:

One of my favorites friendship stories is about my relationship with Chris. She moved into our area and went to the same church I did. I'd seen her around, but I had never spoken to her. I heard through other friends that Chris was awesome--a homemaker from heaven, a talented seamstress, a great cook. She and her husband built their own home and didn't even have a mortgage. Her four children were all honor students. Did I mention that she was nominated for Mother of the Year in our state, and was a slim size four?

I hated her...and I'd never even spoken to her.

I guess the feeling was mutual because she never spoke to me either. Several months after she moved to our town we were thrown into a project together involving taking a youth group from our church to summer camp. We had a meeting together with several other adults and proceeded with arrangements for the outing.

At that time, I was married and had four children. I was still active in sports and that summer I was playing in a ladies softball league. One night, while running to second base, I heard something snap and I went down for the count. I had broken my Achilles' tendon.

A few days later, Chris dropped by to bring me the notes from our previous meeting, (I'm sure she must have typed them at 80 words a minute!) She saw me lying on the couch with my leg in a cast, offered her condolences and left. An hour later she returned, tapped on the door and then walked in so that I wouldn't have to get up. She brought poppy seed chicken, which I'd never eaten before and is still one of my favorites, homemade bread, a stack of books, and a cross-stitch kit. Now, I have no problem eating, and I know how to read, but cross-stitch?"

Chris recognized my dismay and proceeded to teach me to cross-stitch. Since that first piece I have finished hundreds of cross-stitch patterns. I love to stitch. It soothes me. Twenty years later Chris and I sit on the deck at my home overlooking the Snake River in Idaho and cross-stitch. We have been through many crises and joys together. We have laughed and cried, pondered and screamed. Chris is still a wonderful cook and I am not. She is a thousand things that I am not, but do you know what? I am a thousand things she is not, and maybe that is why our friendship works so well. That and the fact someone was brave *enough to step out of her comfort zone long enough to help a virtual stranger in need.*

Once a week, if each one of us reached out to someone different than ourselves and made a new friend, we could literally change the world. If only a thousand women decided to do this once a week for 52 weeks we could create 52,000 new friendships in one year and the repercussions would be tremendous. If this continued beyond that year it could eventually bring about world peace.

__I am only one, but I am one. I cannot do everything, but I can do something. And I will not let what I cannot do interfere with what I can do. ~Edward Everett Hale__

Chapter 7 - I Shouldn't have Spent that Much Money on Shoes!

So why did you do it?

Get rid of the unnecessary guilt in your life. There is a difference between making a mistake and ignoring the guilt, or in doing something to get rid of the guilt. The past is gone, whining, crying, complaining and constantly using it to excuse your present actions will never change the past. Decide what to do with it and move on. Your shoebox isn't big enough to carry guilt bricks in it.

Lyn:

Guilt and money go together like bread and butter.

I will feel so guilty if I buy these shoes but..." I say to myself, "they're red!"

Then I tell myself, "How can I resist? Aren't I worth it?"

I continue to argue with the voice in my head.

"That pair of shoes would feed ten homeless people for a week."

Okay, so this once I put them back. Then on the way home I start to feel guilty about not buying the shoes. Shouldn't I be braver and kinder to myself? If I don't respect and love myself enough to buy a lousy pair of shoes, who will?

I discussed this with Janie and she told me that some guilt is healthy. It's what we do with that guilt that disables us.

Janie:

All of the emotions inside of us were put there for a reason: guilt, joy, sorrow, happiness, fear, love, etc. They all have a purpose.

Take love for example: If we didn't experience love I doubt our species would be very prolific. Why on earth would you have kids if you didn't feel love? After you had that first child, the workload, the inconvenience, and the monetary commitment would stifle any desire to ever have a second one. Children especially the newborn kind foster the emotion of unconditional love.

Every emotion generates some kind of cause and effect.

Learning to discipline the emotions inside of us for our greater good, happens through our past experiences, trial and error, and watching others.

Society has erroneously labeled emotions as either "good" or "bad." The truth is each emotion is both good and bad depending on how it is used.

Guilt works like the signpost at a European intersection. A person reads the signpost pointing the observer to many different destinations. The traveler decides which direction will be the best road to take in order to arrive in a timely manner. If this traveler ignores the signpost or takes a different route than the direct road leading to her final destination a feeling of guilt causes her to stop at the next intersection for another chance to read the signs and question if she needs a course correction. The problem comes when instead of choosing a course correction and moving on, the person is so distraught over making a wrong choice that she pulls up the signpost and insists on carrying it with her. Very quickly that signpost becomes so burdensome that she can't do anything else until be she puts the darn thing down. And once it's been removed from the place it belongs the directional information is no longer correct.

Guilt is the built in mechanism that regulates our own private value system. It is the system of what we determine to be appropriate or inappropriate behavior. When we cross the line of what we believe to be inappropriate, the guilt mechanism kicks in. That's what keeps us paying our house and car payments, and buying groceries to feed our children instead of spending all of our money on the latest gizzy widget that catches our eye.

Guilt is the barometer that causes us to stop and make a judgment call. The problem comes when guilt becomes the governing factor over our lives.

We know from the surveys we have taken of women all over the world (if you want to see or participate in that survey contact us at sistersofthesole.blogspot.com and we will send you a copy.) that there are a few of you who don't feel guilty when you take time or spend money on yourself. (Yes, ladies, it's true, we found a few of you.) By the way, out of those few women who felt no guilt, none of them were mothers. This is sure to make you stop and think and we will discuss this fact at length later on. Basically it boils down to... the more choices you have to make, the more chances you have to feel guilty.

Lyn:

Getting behind on your bills is something many of us have experience with. Let's say a monthly payment--a big payment. Your mate has put you in charge of this responsibility and you have fallen behind. Guilt sets in...the last thing you want is for your partner to find out.

"He will kill me!"

"He will leave me!"

"He will have a heart attack and die!"

"He works so hard for our family it would just crush him to know I haven't kept up on things."

Ask yourself realistically what will happen when he finds out?

(Note: If you are married to a physically abusive spouse then we urge you to seek help through one of the many organizations designed to assist you with this serious issue.)

Nine times out of ten the worst he will do is yell... a lot.

Can you take that?

After the yelling, the two of you will sit down and discuss where the money went, how you are going to fix the crisis, and what you are going to change, so that it doesn't happen again.

Yes, you may have to tighten your budget for a while and he will probably be angry for a few days because you didn't tell him sooner, (before he went out and bought that motorcycle), but the two of you will solve the problem together.

This conversation may be the hardest one you have ever worked through in your entire life, or you may realize that this issue is nothing compared to other ones you have already dealt with. Whatever the outcome this is one of those times when you must solve the problem together.

I remember one time early in my first marriage. I somehow got five house payments behind. I had not spent the money frivolously. All of it had gone for other bills, food, or obligations for our four children, nevertheless, we were behind and the mortgage company wanted their money NOW! I looked under every proverbial rock I could find. I did not want my poor husband who was working overtime to make ends meet, to worry.

He was a gentle giant, so I knew he would not yell, which would have been easier for me to take. He would sulk. He would be so distraught he wouldn't eat. He would sleep a lot more, mope around the house, sigh deeply, and look at me with those Bambi eyes brimming with unshed tears and put a "for sale" sign on the front lawn.

I tried everything in my power to borrow the money without him knowing, but in the end I had no other choice than to tell him. Now, as a writer of fiction, I would like to fabricate some fairytale ending and tell you he reacted totally different than I had expected, but in fact, he reacted exactly how I described. I still remember thirty years later his first words to me. "Oh honey, how could you have let this happen?"

The question and the way he said it ripped me apart. I felt terrible enough. It was as if he thought I had joyfully used that money for hot fudge sundaes and dollar bills for male strippers! How could I?

I swallowed a gulp of pride the size of a watermelon and let him soak in the dreaded knowledge that I had held to myself for months. People may tell you that sharing your pain with others makes it easier, but that is not always the case, especially if you are the one who is causing the pain. In this case it would have been easier to keep the secret.

After the initial shock wore off, he started asking questions. I was not only prepared with details of what we owed, but with several ideas of how to remedy the problem. (This is an essential step when this problem occurs.) We then sat down as a couple with a crisis and came up with a plan. Together we figured out our problem and we set some new rules.

I would not keep money issues from him just because I did not like his reaction to problems.

He would take a more active part in knowing what our expenses were and where the money was actually going so there would be no big surprises.

Sometimes we need to analyze what we are so afraid of when it comes to financial abundance. God loves us. He wants us to be happy. He lives in abundance so why wouldn't he want the same for us?

Anything that consumes our thoughts and energy becomes our reality. If we are constantly worrying about our lack of money we will end up manifesting exactly what we don't want...scarcity. When we live in thankfulness for everything we have: our families, our homes, our health, our jobs, etc. and then ask God to provide financial security, He will help us see opportunities where we may be able to increase our net worth. The more abundant thinking you do the more abundance will come into your life.

Another part of the guilt cycle is trying to accuse somebody else of causing the problem. This is a total waste of time. Blaming others for your problems or blaming somebody else for what has happened blows a huge hole in positive energy. Even if the person is guilty, the first response of human behavior is to put up a defense. So now you have to climb over some great brick wall of resistance before you can address what needs to happen before you can fix the situation.

Janie:

One day in the middle of an argument for some strange reason Robert and I stopped and stepped out of the emotion of the moment to analyze it objectively. We discovered we were spending/wasting time and energy assessing blame to the appropriate person over whatever the trouble was. We began to laugh at ourselves. Once a mistake is made it really doesn't matter who was at fault. Assessing guilt does not fix the problem and it never changes the fact that there is still a problem to solve.

Using our resources of time and energy to solve the problem at hand is much more efficient. But then there was still the issue of blame.... For some reason the human way of thinking needs to blame someone or something in order to move to the next stage of problem solving. I came up with a great solution.... "From this point forward," I said, "EVERYTHING will be MY Fault."

It worked.

Why?

Because it was so ludicrous. Everybody knows that 'Everything' could not possibly be my fault including things that happened when I was not anywhere near the event. Because of this attitude I adopted, it has become the family joke. It adds humor and levity to whatever the problem is. We never waste time talking about 'who did it.' Whenever we are suddenly faced with some kind of dilemma, I say something like, "Oh no... what have I done this time? Or "It's my fault I did it." Sometimes I add to the ridiculous nature of accepting guilt by saying something like, "I tried all day to think of something really stupid to do that would make everybody angry and this was the best thing I could come up with."

The guilty person can now help work out the problem in a positive way rather than spending half an hour defending the stupid mistake while nothing is resolved.

Side issues can be handled privately if it involves a child that needs reproof or if there are deeper elements to be addressed. The main problem becomes a non-emotional situation to be overcome by everybody. The details usually take care of themselves.

Guilt over a variety of topics have been discussed in our survey we will list a few and you can see if any of these ring true with you.

The four main areas of guilt are:

Money: spending, not spending, making, not making.

Time: Not enough for others, not enough for self, poor use of.

Health: exercise, eating habits, addictions, illness.

Relationships.

All of these issues are addressed in some way in various locations in this book, so hopefully armed with this information and encouragement, you don't have to carry guilt bricks, guilt signposts, or guilty burdens any longer.

Stress Busters:

Stress is debilitating. We want to help you relieve stress for you and your loved ones. We hope we don't make you angry by suggesting that you cause your own stress. (Yeah right, try telling that to my friend who just found out that her husband has cancer). The idea that stress is self-imposed is a hard pill to swallow.

Janie:

A few years ago I was in Holland with my husband attending his Aunt's funeral. At home in the United States my parents were involved in a serious automobile accident. My mother suffered broken ribs, ankle, collarbone, and a broken neck. She was placed into intensive care in critical condition.

I was having a relaxing get-away, and renewing of acquaintances with distant family members. I felt no stress whatsoever until the phone call came describing the circumstances at home.

Now I am not suggesting that you should just ignore serious events and responsibilities, but I am showing you that you choose your stress levels by how you react to the situations in your life.

Lyn:

Stress is a common buzz-word in today's vocabulary and is a symptom of our lifestyles and our society. I truly believe that our ancestors, with all their struggles and pain in the early years of this country would not want to trade places with us and the stresses we live with today.

However, even though we experience stress daily in many different ways, we know that it is important to reduce that stress. If we do not learn how to lower stress in our lives there will be more and more of us that will snap from the strain either physically or mentally.

Recently I was in New York City for several days. Although I love New York and all its vibrant energy, I would have a difficult time living there without finding myself a haven to retreat to--a quiet place where I felt protected from the world around me.

We all need a place or haven where one can retreat. In battle a place of retreat is essential to regroup, recharge, and renew the strategies. The same thing is true in our lives.

Your haven can be anywhere and any size. Let's see if we can create the perfect spot just for you. This will be fun. First let's create your space on paper. This practice alone can be enjoyable and very relaxing. It is one of my favorite stress busters because you can experience all the emotions of actual ownership and location, with your paper and a good shot of imagination.

Imagine a perfect space for you to relax in. This can be a room, a cottage, a cabin, or a mansion, whatever fits your personality. Ask yourself what you would have in your room. Think of every detail. What type of furniture would you have, an overstuffed chair or a chaise lounge? Would there be a fireplace? If so, what type? How about a pool outside your window? Would you have a bookcase full of books? If so, who would the authors of those books be? What kind of music would be playing? What type of flowers, paintings, candles, scents? Take your time with these details. Think it through. There is no hurry. The joy is in creating.

This project can be ongoing. Set it out before you. Put the project in an easily accessible location but not necessarily where anybody else will see it or that it will be in the way of daily living. If it is close at hand it can be comforting to you. A sort of mental retreat each time you look at it, and as you find things that appeal to you they can be added.

Now look through magazines and catalogs of any kind that interest you. Shop through the pictures without spending a dime. You can be as extravagant or frugal as you choose. Cut out every thing you want for your perfect stress free room. Put it in your Joy In The Journey Journal. You will find as you go out into the real world and as you can afford it, you might start to purchase those things or something comparable. It doesn't matter if you can't do it all right now or even in the next few years. It doesn't matter if you change your mind, just looking through your journal can bring you comfort.

Stress comes from our minds. Over and over again our brain tells us how life should be and because it is not exactly that way, we create our own stress.

So let's get to the list of stress busters and if you've got a good way that we have missed please send it to us and we will pass it on to the rest of you.

Make your muscles move. Just making the decision to do something... anything, it doesn't really matter what it is, it will begin to restore a feeling of control and your stress will lessen.

Breathing Techniques. A simple form of meditation is taking a long slow breath, counting slowly until you cannot take in any more air. Hold this breath for the same count as you had breathing it in. Slowly exhale for the same count. Concentrate on nothing but your breathing.

Be Still. Practice being still. Observe your surroundings, no criticism, no judgment, just observation.

Exercise, running, walking, aerobic, yoga, sports, tennis, golf, swimming, dancing etc. Physicians have suggested physical exercise as an inexpensive stress reliever.

Star Gazing. It is comforting at night to see how organized and constant God is in His heaven. It reminds us that He does not leave us alone when it is dark.

Crafts: knitting, crochet, scrapbooking, cross-stitch. There is something soothing about the rhythm of creating something beautiful.

Playing Games: Suduko, puzzles, cards, chess, Mah Jong, Some people feel that games are a waste of time, but we found in our survey that many women are able to relax when they play games and that it gives their mind and body a much needed rest.

Take a nap.

Gardening: Lyn has a sign in her garden that says: "In my garden, the answers come." And it is so true. She says her mind calms, her breathing slows, she breathes in fresh air. She hears nature and it heals her.

Bird watching.

Walk through a park or through a forest

Go to water: the ocean, a river, a lake, a waterfall, a shower, a bathtub

Visit an art gallery

Read: About era's you love, places you yearn to visit, novels you have longed to read, revisit novels you have enjoyed before.

Read out loud to a child or the elderly or even your spouse. Some of my fondest memories are my husband and I reading books out loud together.

Volunteer to help people learn how to read.

Listen to a book on CD or an electronic player.

Gaze into a fire.

Watch fish swim in an aquarium.

Cook or Bake.

Paint

Write: your history, keep a journal, write to relieve stress.

Take up photography.

Spend time with a pet.

Pick flowers, arrange flowers, take pictures of flowers, paint pictures of flowers. When you take the time to study flowers and their beauty you are looking into the eyes of God. We can learn much about our own nature from the growth and beauty of a flower. You can relieve stress this way.

Play music: whether you play an instrument or simply listen, music soothes the savage beast.

Take a hot shower or a soothing bath.

Clean something: Pick a closet or room that you have been procrastinating about cleaning and just dig in. Soon your task will be done and your stress will be lower and the best part of the process is you now have an area organized that brought you only stress before. Simply standing there looking at the finished product will give a feeling of peace and renewed energy.

Get away: Take a ride through the countryside or make a weekend out of it going to the beach or a campground.

Pamper yourself with a pedicure, manicure, or get your hair done.

Work: Do some kind of physical labor, the harder the better.

Lyn:

One of my best friends was a former Buddhist Monk. Every time I had a problem I would take it to David and he always gave me the same advice. "Remember the old Chinese saying I taught you? Chop wood, carry water and your answers will come."

Write a letter, not an e-mail, a real sit down with a pen and paper message to someone you care about and let him or her know how you feel.

Skateboard, ride a bike, skate, swing, sleigh ride, ski, snowboard

Go to the movie, hold hands with your lover. Take kids to a movie and love it right along with them. Go alone and enjoy the solitude of watching a movie by yourself.

Eat popcorn

Eat to get and stay healthy.

Call an old friend.

Color with crayons:

(**Lyn**: *This is still a stress buster for me and my grandkids. They love to see me doing something that they love to do, and you wouldn't believe some of the conversations we have!*)

Laugh: Don't lose your sense of humor and if, by some chance, you have lost it, find it again. Find at least one thing each day to laugh about. Laughing improves your well being and health.

Build something: A dollhouse, a model car, a bench, or refurbish a piece of furniture.

Play dolls: Comb their hair, change their clothes, imagine their lives.

Lyn: *As a girl my friends and I used to play dolls for hours and I don't remember any stress.*

Rake leaves or mow the lawn.

Volunteer

Donate items to charity.

Take a cruise.

Join a club. A book club, The Red Hat's Society, P.T.O. Networking with others of like interest can be fun and empowering.

Study something you have always been fascinated with: The Ming Dynasty, The Civil War, Culinary Art. We all have areas of interest and sometimes we don't even know why we are drawn to certain things.

Take time to explore, and while you are learning you just might discover something new about yourself. Maybe you will acquire a skill or gain information that will be useful at some point in the future. You cannot guess where the path will lead.

Watch people: especially children.

Lyn: *One of my favorite things to do is sit in my grandson, Cru's, bedroom and watch him play. When I feel anxious and overwhelmed with life, I watch Cru play. He loves my undivided attention and it isn't long before I find myself breathing more easily, and evenly, and smiling, and laughing joyously. My daughter uses this technique with her children as well.*

Sing: Singing works for every mood and emotion. Even your breathing has to improve in order to sing. By the way, you do not have to have a great voice to sing. And you don't have to have an audience either.

Dance: If you are good or talented at dancing go back to it or continue on. If you are not, take a go at it. Even if you wouldn't be caught dead letting anybody see you dance, take the opportunity when nobody is watching to let it go. Put on some music and dance your little heart out. It feels great.

Listen to a baby laugh.

Lyn: *I was in Mississippi for a few weeks and my family was two thousand miles away. One day when I was feeling homesick I received a call from my daughter. "Listen to this, Mom" and then I heard my three-month-old granddaughter giggle for the first time. Over and over again her clear beautiful giggle rang true to my heart. I found myself grinning like a goosed duck and laughing along with her. It changed my outlook for a whole week.*

Cuddle with a person, or pet, or even a soft fleece throw, warm it in the dryer and fix yourself a cup of something steamy to go with it.

Get enough sleep: There is all sorts of information to help you determine why you cannot sleep. Find out what your problem is and take care of it. Sleep affects every other aspect of your life. Often you simply need to be more physically active to obtain that good night's rest. Our bodies have to have something to rest from. Working in the yard or scrubbing a floor in the evening is a great way to exert those muscles so they can more effectively rest a few hours later. If you can't turn your mind off try the breathing exercise we gave you back at suggestion #2. Refuse to allow yourself to think about anything but your breathing, counting, and relaxing.

Self-Hypnosis: Once again, there is a lot of information out there. Find out what works for you.

Positive self-talk

Compliment others, but be sincere.

Praise yourself out loud and those you care about.

Invite someone lonely to dinner.

Eat Chocolate.

Write a thank you note.

Read uplifting or spiritual material.

Meditate.

Pray.

Talk out loud to God and your angels and ask for their help.

Write a mantra for yourself and recite it out loud daily, or when you can't sleep.

Recite affirmations.

Choose a task that you have been dreading and do it.

Lyn: *Mine is sorting and paying bills. I will do almost anything to get out of this job. In fact, that is why I am writing this right now. So think of the task you detest--cleaning the fridge, toilet, the upholstery in your car, a room in your basement, the cat mess in the garage. (I know you have a couple of these.) Put on your rubber gloves, a clothes pin on your nose and get er' done! I have a pile of bills in front of me right now, my rubber gloves are on and the clothespin is on my nose. I can guarantee that if you will tackle one of these jobs, you will feel five years younger and ten pounds lighter.*

Make a list of your stressful situations. This will help you to find what it is that creates the problem areas for you. Now take these areas one at a time and find a solution, one that is tailor made just for you. It does not matter if it is unconventional or seems to be silly. If it works for you then go for it.

Chapter 8 - Want New Shoes?
Make a List

When you really want something in your life, write it down. If you write it down, you own it. Write it like it is already yours, and you are in the place you want to be.

When you write something down it solidifies it into your psyche. Subconsciously you begin to attract the elements of what you have written into your life. Sometimes you are not even aware the things you have written are coming to you.

Do everything in your power to achieve what you want. Work hard. Time and circumstances will dictate the ways and means that what you have written will come to you, so be ready, aware and patient. Very soon that $200.00 pair of dreamed of shoes or dreamed of peace of mind will be yours.

Find yourself a notebook to use only for dreaming. Date each entry. The date is important to monitor your timeline. Remember the song that says, **Sometimes I thank God for unanswered prayers?** Well the same concept applies here. You probably will not get everything you write about and that is a good thing. It is kind of like the little kid who wants to eat the whole quart of ice cream and Mom knows it will make him sick. God knows what you really need and/or can handle. But still, you have to ask. Dreams are vital to your feelings of hope, and your belief in good things to come.

Make dream lists. Write down your deepest desires. It does not matter if it seems silly or trite. If you feel it today, write it down. Often seeing something in writing changes your perspective on it. It is good to get it out of your thought process and onto paper. This frees up your brain to think about other stuff. Many times after you write something down you realize you really are not all that interested in having whatever it is you wrote about. If it is innocuous, leave it. If it is something you would rather nobody ever saw, tear it up. You wrote yourself through it and maybe that is all you needed to do. Now you can get rid of it and unclutter your mind, no longer wasting time wishing for something you really don't want.

On the other hand occasionally when you write your desires, passions, or needs, the possibilities grow. You begin to see doors you could open on the way to find ways you can have your wants fulfilled. Opportunities manifest themselves to you in ways you never imagined. Writing things down solidifies to yourself the level of your commitment to whatever it is.

Besides all the analytical serious stuff, it is fun. Dreaming is healthy. It is a form of escape from the chaotic, or humdrum, or problem driven circumstances of a person's everyday life.

Janie:

I love perusing the pages of catalogues. For ten minutes I can own whatever I see.

Your mind has the ability to create the exact feelings, hormones, and endorphins from mentally claiming ownership of something as it does from actually acquiring the desired thing.

My favorite part of virtual ownership is that it is guilt free. It costs you nothing but a little time and imagination. It won't offend or impede on anyone else. It does not affect the budget, and it makes a person feel good.

This concept works especially well if the person in reality has the money to buy the desired item, but chooses not to. You see the power of money is in having it. As long as you have the money you can mentally spend it a hundred different ways. It's good to use over and over again. However, once you actually spend the money, it's gone. And usually the item loses its interest and/or value rather quickly because the enticement is in the desire to acquire, not in the real ownership.

Virtual ownership also works well when you don't have the money to genuinely own the thing you desire. When you allow yourself to mentally own something and really put yourself into the ownership realm it satisfies those yearnings. Your body goes through the exact same emotion base as if in reality you held in your hand the new car keys, house keys, plane ticket, or some other item. And look at this aspect...your dreams are maintenance free, no taxes, yard work, or tires to rotate. In other words, you have all the fun and none of the responsibility.

For a number of years my daughter and I owned a business together. Part of this job was to decorate the Parade of Homes house my husband built each year. It was a sort of temporary ownership that satisfied the decorating bug. We could in a limited way fulfill that dream of buying the latest greatest, or having the newest style, many of us are susceptible to. In this experience I realized to a greater degree that the virtual ownerships I had experienced from my 'catalogue fantasies' were every bit as fulfilling and less cumbersome than the real thing.

Writing is a very tactile experience. It physically involves more than just your mind. It incorporates a cooperation with your eyes, arms, hands, and possibly other body parts as you sit, stand, or lie down while you write. It is soothing to hold a pen, pencil, or other writing utensil, form the letters, and write the words. Sliding your hand across the paper records and reminds the brain of certain feelings both past and present. This exercise performed on a keyboard can also have a sensual fulfillment although it generally is more pronounced during the actual hand to paper process.

Dr. James Pennebaker Ph.D. from the University of Texas at Austin, has published works exploring the links between a person writing things down and improved mental and/or physical health. It is now documented in this and other studies. Writing is healing and healthy.

Janie:

My husband had a heart attack and died in my car on the way to the hospital and then was revived in a very dramatic way. The ensuing emergencies, medical procedures, and problems that arose over the next few weeks concerning his health and future, and the eventual outcome of it all traumatized our entire family. It also affected many people in our church and surrounding community.

I found myself reliving the details while I washed dishes, performed other menial tasks, or drove from point A to point B. For some reason my brain was afraid I would forget the details and so I had to rehearse everything mentally over and over again. Desperate to find some relief from these flashbacks I began writing in minute detail every aspect of the experience. Day after day I would sit down and write another episode of the event until I reached a point where I no longer had to think about it anymore. Once it was all set down on paper my mind relaxed and I could let it go.

Each day as I finished writing I slid the paper under the oversized desk pad so I could run in and add details here and there without having to get things out or put things away. It was a hectic time with the health concerns of my husband and filled with my ten children who were all ages from three years old to twenty-two years, and included all of their goings and comings. Unbeknownst to me my older children were secretly pulling out the papers each day and reading what I had written. It was as therapeutic for them to read it as it was for me to write it.

When I stopped writing for a few days, the older children came to me and asked if the story was finished. It was then that I realized they had been sneaking in the room every day to see what I had written.

Although this form of writing is not exactly the same thing as making a list or writing down goals, dreams, and suggestions, the writing of the event gave Janie ownership and validation of what happened and the role she and others played in the eventual outcome. Once she had gone through the safe comforting feeling of controlling the event on paper she had subdued the monster. It was now caged on the paper. She could visit it any time she wanted, but it could not hurt her anymore, and she was free to let it go from her daily life.

Lyn:

Similar to Janie's catalog surfing, I spent time with magazines in the early days of raising my family. I did not have the money to buy the things I liked, nor did I have the body to wear the clothes I liked. None of that kept me from dreaming. My magazine pile was huge. I knew I couldn't keep all of them. So one day I decided to sort through the stack and throw out the ones I did not need. Actually I didn't need any of them, but in each one I'd kept was something I loved; a cozy cottage room, a sofa, chair, hairstyle, dress, garden, flower, body, or a place that I wanted to visit someday.

I bought a big old-fashioned scrapbook and I started cutting things out and gluing the dream bits into it. Once or twice a month while the family was busy with a movie, I would sit down with my pictures and cut and paste.

There is something soothing about these activities. Your mind rests. I found myself transported for a few seconds to that bedroom in soft lavender or that front porch under a giant oak. This experience was in the late seventies long before I had ever heard of Visualization Boards or even scrapbooking as it is today. This project had no rhyme or reason to it, I know what a professional scrap collection of today looks like, and my daughters-in-law are experts. This project... my project was simple but nevertheless rewarding.

Every time I entered new pictures I looked through the previous pages and enjoyed a moment in each scene, each chair, each dress. Each entry spoke to my soul or touched me in some small way. On one page there is a picture of a couple holding hands, she is smiling up at him, and he is hiding a white teddy bear with a red heart on its chest. Other pages display a photo of a rustic cabin in the woods, a bubble bath in a claw foot tub, a red sofa, a chocolate brownie, a beach scene and an aquamarine stone to match the ocean's perfect color. I filled the entire book with pictures and dreams and when it was full I began another.

A few years ago I discovered that first scrapbook while in the process of moving to River's Edge. I sat down and enjoyed gazing at each page, each item, and the feeling it had given me on that day long ago when I pasted it there. Even after all those years, I still loved everything in those pages from lilacs to amethysts.

What truly startled me was the realization that I had, during the past 30 years, acquired everything in that book! In fact that very Valentine's Day Butch had given me a white teddy bear with a red heart on his chest! He had never seen or heard of my book nor had I mentioned to him my love for teddy bears.

Here is the point--what we put into our minds we create---good or bad. If I had known how it worked I perhaps would have chosen a little more carefully on some things, but on second thought maybe not. I also have in that first book a picture of a little girl in a ballerina costume, her dark hair piled on top of her head. That wish came true more than once with a daughter and more recently, granddaughters.

Dreams do come true.

Writing things down and putting them on paper or on a visualization board places images in your brain. These subconscious images work to secretly influence your actions. Your subconscious is generally very patient. It waits and watches for the right moment to urge you into an action that in some way will fulfill the expectation you placed there long ago.

Janie:

My daughter, Rachel, was cleaning out her house prior to a move to another state for her husband's work. In a box of stuff left over from her high school days, Rachel found a sealed envelope. It was an assignment from ten years before. She had to write a letter to herself describing 100 things she wanted to do in her lifetime. Once she had completed the assignment, she sealed it in an envelope. She never thought of it again until this very moment. It was such a forgotten memory that she had to open the envelope and read the letter to remind herself of the assignment. She was stunned as she read the letter to herself and realized she had completed nearly all of the things in the letter.

When telling me about the experience Rachel said a lot of the things she had written were unusual or seemingly impossible for someone who was, at the time she wrote it, one of ten children, very limited in income, growing up in a rural Utah town.

A few of the things accomplished on her list were: Graduate from college; achieve more that one kind of degree; go to New York for something important; live in another state; successfully own and operate a business; enter and be successful in some kind of competition; travel to Europe, marry and have a family.

It was her opinion that carefully thinking through her desires and writing them down on the list placed those ideas into her subconscious and as opportunities arose, she was compelled to do what was written even though consciously she had forgotten about the letter.

The same day she showed me her letter, I walked into a bookstore and one of the featured books I saw was entitled, "Write it Down, Make it Happen." by Henriette Anne Klauser. Of course I had to buy the book.

I do believe that which you send out into the universe returns to you.

Be careful about your list making.

Lists are very good tools for remembering things.

On the other hand lists can be very destructive to self-esteem.

When your shopping list says to buy milk, eggs, and bread and you don't have time to shop, or you change your mind and buy apples, hot dogs and orange juice, rarely do you consider yourself a complete failure, or a hopeless wreck of a person who has failed miserably in basic grocery shopping. For some reason, however, when you make of list of things you 'should' do, for example: exercise 20 minutes; read to my children; call my mother-in-law; or pay the bills, and you don't finish this list, you berate and judge yourself as lacking in moral character. You have let yourself down, in other words…. In your mind and thinking… You have failed.

List making should be taken in the context of what it is… A list. It is not a life sentence. It is not a definitive statement of character. It certainly is not set in stone.

Janie:

A long time ago I was working with a woman who wrote down what she had to do every day and then succumbed to extreme depression when her daily routine was constantly interrupted by all her children and their lives. She never finished any of her lists. She felt like a disorganized failure. This sense of accomplishment seemed vital to her personal well-being so I made a suggestion. I told her not to make a list for tomorrow. Instead of starting the day with a list when she went to bed she should write down everything she did that was positive during that day and then put a check mark next to it as though she had written it there and it had been there all day and now she was crossing it off of her to do list.

She told me later that she had adopted this new practice and she was no longer depressed. She also said that her productivity had gone up tremendously because now she hurried through one task after another as she envisioned how many things she would get to 'check' on her bedtime list.

You are the master of the lists you make. Be careful not to become the slave to them. They are not human and as such they do not harbor any human compassion, emotions, or abilities. It is not a crime to rip one up and throw it away.

Both of us often make lists for various reasons and then burn them. Awhile ago we wrote down a list of things we thought might possibly be holding our progress back. We ripped the lists into small pieces and sent them out into the ocean on the shore of Agadir, Morocco. The symbolism of this for us was… This was far enough away from where we lived in the United States that the bad kharma of thinking that there were things holding us back would never return.

A list is a tool, a helpful tool. Writing things on paper is also helpful and healing. Practice using list making and writing things down in a productive way. Feel how empowering it is to be in control of your destiny even if it is only on a piece of paper. It is the first step to controlling the direction of, the understanding of, and the divine decree of, all the rest.

Chapter 9 - Wear the Soft Soled Shoes

Going into the quiet place calms the Sole (Soul).

Today there is a media blitz about everything. The cacophony of television, radio, movies, and earphones connected to every kind of sound device, cell phones, speakers, and voices, dulls our senses. It all becomes an unconscious drone in the background of our lives. Noise deafens our intuition, and demeans our intelligence.

The media myth purports that people are currently more connected and more informed. Pay attention here. Most of what you see is the smoke and mirrors effect of the olden days' traveling side shows. Contrary to the inference that news is happening every minute of every day the reality is there is only so much of what is happening in any given day that can be reported. On some days there is more and on other days there is a little less. Each newscaster is vying for the position of presenting the same story over and over again in the most dynamic way possible to increase his or her ratings.

Years ago the only means of communication other than face-to-face was with the written word and it was difficult to transport. Samuel Finley Breese Morse invented a telegraph and a mode of transporting signals in the form of dots and dashes to pass information more quickly and efficiently. Alexander Graham Bell followed up with his invention of the telephone. Quickly the need for people to talk voice to voice but not face to face with each other facilitated putting more than one person on those very limited resources. This resulted in a concept of 'party lines.' If a person wanted to make a phone call he or she would first pick up the phone and check to see if anybody else was using the shared line. On a party line if each of the people sharing the line picked up his or her phone at the same time they could all talk together with each other.

From the party line we evolved to fiber optics, computers, e-mail, cell phones, and ipads and ipods.

At last we have come full circle. Texting and instant messaging is nothing but a more advanced process of the telegraph's Morse code. Beyond that we have again advanced or returned to the process called 'Twittering, Instagram, Snap-Chat,' and whatever else is the newest latest, greatest, and fastest method currently taking over these innovations with some other kind of instant communication." This is essentially the same idea as a party line. People send out a communication that can be immediately seen and responded to by all the followers of the sender. It is a sophisticated party line. Our needs do not change… only our toys and the means to fulfill those needs.

The number one difference between now and then is that yesterday a person had to seek out the means of functioning the noise of communication. Now a person has to seek out a place where she can shut the noise off.

Finding quiet time, a quiet place, and a quiet mind is a secret that enables us to walk with confidence through many of the challenges facing us. When we do this our inner capacity has been fortified, rested, and rejuvenated. We are more in touch with private strengths, talents, and capabilities.

Find your quiet mind.

Lyn:

Alone Time

Why is being alone such a rarity? Why do we feel we have to lie and make excuses when we what we want is to simply be alone for an hour, a day, or even a week?

I was in my thirties before I ever spent a week alone. It was mid-October. I left my family at home and went to my parents cabin in the mountains to write. I didn't know a single person in the area and I wanted it that way. I had no plans other than to read, write, rest, and think.

The members of my family reacted in various ways to my decision. My children thought it was cool. When their dad was in charge they had a blast! My husband felt deserted and threatened. My parents worried that something was wrong in my marriage and my husband's parents were absolutely appalled, thinking me a terrible wife and mother. Keep in mind that my husband took off with friends several times a year to go hunting, and no one had a first thought about that let alone a second thought.

I was gone five days. I didn't see one soul for those five days. I worked hard and did everything I intended to do and nothing more than that. But if you had spoken to my husband or his parents you would have thought I had been gone a year!

I ask my question another way--why do we have to make excuses for wanting to heal ourselves through solitude?

Since that first time, I have had many alone times. Some of them have been self-imposed through decisions I made and some, my husband's death for example, were not of my choosing. However, even in the times when it has not been my choice, I have been able to survive the experiences because I could go back in my mind to a gentler time when I was at peace in my aloneness.

I have my own little cabin now in the same mountains in Idaho where I first found that solitude. On my mountain I feel safe even though many wild animals trudge through my property. I feel small and insignificant as I lay on a blanket in the midst of towering pine trees. I don't feel anxiety at my smallness. I feel pleasure, knowing I am not in charge. I feel that a power much greater than mine is in control, and that I do not have to fix everything. I am reminded I am only in charge of myself and that is a good thing. I feel protected and surrounded by God and my angels. I am not only okay alone, I actually like my own company and it all began that October so long ago. What a kinder, gentler world it would be if everyone had a private quiet retreat of his or her own.

I think of my cozy place as a gas station. I sometimes get drained of fuel in my world of family, friends, career, house and yard work etc. These responsibilities keep my tank ever depleted. But every time I leave the forest I am once more full and ready to give of myself to others. I have to be careful not to let my tank get below the quarter mark, for I find myself becoming abrupt, rude, tired, restless, argumentative and so forth.

Everyone needs a quiet place, even if it's only in our minds. I believe that crimes and tragedies occur when a person's tank is empty. We must first recognize the signs and then find something or some place to refill our tank.

Janie:

Interest rates soared, my husband's construction and real estate company folded. We lost our business, our home, and our life as we knew it.

My father helped us buy a small home about forty miles away in a rural community. It was built around 1900. My domain left a corporate life and a house of 6,400 square feet with every modern convenience available, to what we affectionately called the money pit. It had 1,250 square feet, one bathroom, and two tiny closets that were each only about two and a half feet wide. The only dishwashers we had avoided the kitchen at all costs and had to be kicked started to work. (Just joking...I never kicked any of my children to make them work; however, I did bribe them a lot.) This home turned out to be both a blessing and a challenge for us and at that time our six children.

Old Mr. Stewart died in the house two years before we purchased it. Nobody else had lived in it. His daughters left behind most of the household accouterments. Since we were totally broke it was a blessing the house had a stove, even if it was manufactured in 1952 (Which was the year I was born. We moved into this house in 1983). We had to take turns holding the oven door shut if we wanted to bake cookies. I set the timer and each kid had to hold the door for two minutes. (Having lots of kids was an advantage here.) If we wanted to bake a roast or casserole we braced a chair up against the handle to hold the door as tightly shut as possible.

In retrospect, even the challenges turned out to be blessings. Our lives slowed down from the frenetic pace of high income living with all the choices and responsibilities attached to that lifestyle. For the kids, and us the adventure of having to create our own entertainment because we could not afford anything else became an exciting journey of discovery. We began finding the quiet places of our lives in the midst of the chaos of a large family with hardly enough places for all of us to sleep, let alone put stuff away.

The house had been part of a farm so there were old abandoned out buildings. We tried our hand at raising a few chickens, and pigs. The kids made spy, science fiction, and fantasy movies in and around the yard. Then they charged the neighbor kids a small fee to come and watch them and buy their homemade popcorn.

We also planted gardens. I kept a log of the prices of produce at the local grocery store and matched them to the harvest out of our garden. At the end of the summer I subtracted the money I put into the garden from the amount I would have spent in the store. Even in the bad weed filled years we still came out ahead.

My garden tending started early in the morning before the kids woke up. In the solitude of sunrises I found peace amongst the peas, hope in the tomatoes, and abundance in the zucchinis. Massaging the vestiges of Mother Earth with my hands and sometimes my whole body, she yielded up her gift of strength and energy. How grateful I was for those quiet moments of rejuvenation.

Amazingly we watched very little television. Once we became reacquainted with each other, we played games, we worked together, and we worked alone. When our now grown children talk of their most cherished memories they center mostly in and around our life 'in the old house.'

And what about relationships?

Have you ever considered it takes some thoughtful meditation to sort out the relationships in your life?

Jot down the names of each person in your immediate surroundings. This list is for people you encounter as part of your life each day. After you make the list touch each name with your pen or pencil and just wait. It is like when you place a computer pointer over an icon and wait for a second or two and the computer reveals some kind of information about that particular icon. It usually tells you why it is there and perhaps what its function is. The same thing will happen in your brain. As your pencil touches that person's name images will begin to form in your brain. Your body will react to how you feel about that person right this minute. Perhaps you will actually see short video clips of events involving the two of you.

Ponder what is being revealed. Don't criticize yourself. Become an observer. Once you comprehend what your feelings and opinions are then you can act to improve your relationship, know how to help, or how to understand this person.

Move your pencil to the next name and continue. When you do this for the first time, we suggest you put a time limit on your pondering. Keep it short, not longer than a couple of minutes.

Sometimes if you are unfamiliar with how your brain works and you sit on one name for a long time your brain will run amuck. By this we mean that the first impressions are usually productive. The longer you dwell, the brain begins to make stuff up. It is the 'monster in the closet' syndrome.

Don't create a monster that does not exist.

Lyn:

Neighborhood Quiet Time

When my children were young, we lived in a neighborhood with lots of kids. One summer the mothers got together and decided as a neighborhood we would have a "quiet time" between the hours of 1:00 and 3:00 every afternoon. Since all of the kids were usually in and out of each others homes, this would give each mother a much needed rest...or not.

It was left up to the individual mother to decide what she would do in those two hours. I chose to read to my children, or have them read to me, or draw pictures. Sometimes we would make a craft of some sort, or cookies. If you have done any of these activities with kids you know that 'quiet time' is out of the question and you have probably created a huge mess to clean up. That's okay, I was trying to create a unique quiet time, you see. It wasn't quiet in the attitude of no noise but rather in the quietness of separation. It was separation from others, from the world. For two hours it was just me and my children quietly separating ourselves from everything outside.

As I look back on that time, I wonder how it might have been better if I had explained that each one of us (including mom) would find a quiet place in the house or yard and do what they would like to do (within reason) without disturbing others. The kids might have been bored for the first few days until they learned to enjoy their own company, but how might their attitudes have been different if we had tried that?

And what about a father's quiet time? Usually, the father of our family rarely even got to sit down before we had him loaded into the car heading for a ballgame. Meals were eaten on the run and we usually never get home before the ten o'clock news.

Is it any wonder that tempers flare and relationships suffer?

What if we only changed one thing in our lives? What if we afforded others and ourselves one hour of solitude a day, could we change the world? At the very least change our own lives? And after all, isn't that how we begin to make a global change--one life at a time?

Lyn:

When I was a newlywed I went on a hunting trip with my husband. Since I wasn't into hunting, I chose to stay at camp while my husband hunted for a deer with his buddies. Our camp trailer was parked on the grounds of an old weathered farmhouse owned by some friends of ours. The house stood empty for most of the year, but during deer hunting season it filled with family and friends.

While the boys were in the hills, Ruth, the mother of this large clan, had the house to herself. At this time Ruth was old...fifty or so, (several years younger than I am now.) She had raised a large family and was also a schoolteacher. Now I think back on it my intrusion into her world must have been discouraging to say the least. There is no doubt in my mind as I reflect on that trip that she wanted to be alone. In my immature twenty-year-old mind, I could not comprehend why she would want to be alone...all day, with no book or television? Ruth stood for hours wrapped in a ratty old sweater warming herself next to an old coal oil stove. She had a serene quietly content expression on her face.

She listened to me ramble on and on, and I am sure she was greatly relieved when I ventured off to my trailer to read. At the time, I could not understand her actions, but over the years there are times when my world has been spinning out of control, and I have thought of Ruth. I wonder what she must have been thinking. I wonder if she had been listening to me or if she had shut out my ramblings and had retreated to her own world, pasting that sweet listening smile on her face simply for my benefit.

Over the years I have come to understand Ruth's silence that day. I've had times when nothing drastic has happened, but every day life has jerked me one project to the next until I simply had to stop before I tip over. I have also had my own times of muteness when a tragedy has occurred and after many days of shock and weeping I have fallen into a sort of stupor.

A week after my first husband was tragically killed trying to save others in an industrial accident, there was a funereal and he was buried, I retired to my cabin in the woods. I went alone against the concern and wishes of every person that cared for me. I needed to grieve--really grieve--alone. We had been so happy together especially at our cabin and we had spent our last weekend together there.

It was raining when I arrived, a cold grey drizzle that matched my heart. I wrapped myself in a blanket for warmth and comfort and went outside to sit on the porch letting the soft rain weep with me. When I finally went into the cabin, I was shocked to realize I had been sitting in the rain for nine and a half hours.

Recently, I have had days when I realize that in this moment--right now-- nothing is wrong. Everything is okay. It is so rare that I just stop what I am doing, breathe deeply, and do nothing--absolutely nothing. And I thoroughly enjoy doing it. Why are we so afraid of the quiet? Have we filled our lives with so much noise that we can't relax without it?

Have you ever said, or at least thought, "Oh, what I would give for an hour of peace and quiet to myself?" What would you do with that hour? Could you occupy your brain without television, conversation, music or something to read? If you are like most of us you are probably thinking, "Sure I could do that." So we challenge you to try it. And then ask yourself this question again--"Where do your thoughts go when you don't have to think?"

List some of these thoughts in your journal. If they are questions answer them. If they are answers, question why you think of them.

Janie:

It was my oldest daughter's wedding day. The ceremony was held very early in the morning about an hour's drive from our home. The wedding breakfast came after, and then we drove back to our house where we would host a garden reception later in the afternoon and early evening.

If any of you have been involved with a day like this you know how intertwined, busy, and specific all the events are. There are mountains of details to remember, especially if you are doing everything yourself. We usually do them ourselves because we are a big family with many talents... and these events can cost lots of money. We also have a Dad and Husband who cooks, cleans, and caters, besides building houses, so he looks at things like this as a piece of cake... wedding cake to be specific.

For a number of years after this day my daughter and I hosted weddings as a business. We tried to get the people to keep their wedding day as simple as possible and spend their energies enjoying the day. We told each wedding party that something has to go wrong in order to have great memories and stories to tell years later. We gave this advice because of what happened on this, my first daughter's wedding day.

After the ceremony the entire extended family was standing outside and the photographer was going through all kinds of machinations trying to get the group organized and attention focused on him. He wanted to take a couple of family pictures in front of the rock building where the marriage had been performed before the group began dispersing. We obliged him in the way large groups do, moms tagging runaway babies, youth skulking about wanting to get their church clothes off as soon as possible, and the wedding couple so enamored with each other they were oblivious to anything going on around them.

The group gets together all eyes focused on the photographer. It is a large group so the photographer climbs up onto the wall of a rather large fountain. He raises his hand, "Everybody look at me, please," he says. This is followed by his hand waving back and forth. We are attentively following the moving hand. His voice begins to sound like some foreign African chant. "Ohhh, yaaaaa. Okay. Ohhhhhh, Uhhhhhh." He raises one leg. The group smiles dutifully. He must be trying to entertain the young ones, we think.

Then it happens. He wasn't entertaining us after all. He had no thought of trying to keep the attention of the young ones. He was waffling back and forth trying to keep from falling into the fountain. He finally loses his balance all together and falls backwards into this large fountain. On the way down his hand holding the camera opens gently as he descends in what seemed like slow motion and the camera deposited safely on the wall where he had been standing. It was like a well-orchestrated Hollywood stunt.

The group of us was so stunned that for a moment none of us moved. After all we had been admonished not to move no matter what. It was only a split second before we all realized how silly we were and that none of this was part of the photographer's original program.

The men rushed forward and pulled him out of the fountain. He insisted on finishing the photography since the camera had miraculously been preserved. It was hard not giggling as we watched and heard him squishing around snapping bridal shots in his saturated wingtip shoes and full dress suit complete with dripping tie.

Within minutes of the fountain fiasco the clouds rolled in and it began to rain. For the next couple of hours the rain pelted everybody and everything. Great for the farmers, bad for the wedding plans.

At the very moment when we were deciding if we should take the contingency plan of moving to the local church for the reception the rain stopped and immediately the sun began shinning brilliantly through the clouds. The water rose off the sidewalks in light steamy puffs.

We were all back at our house now and the men left to take care of table moving and other manly tasks. The household was all bustling efficiently around with 'the details' which of course, were important.

I happened to glance out of the back window. I called to Rachel, my newly wedded daughter. "Come here a minute," I said. She stopped working in the kitchen and followed me outside. I sat down on a bench and motioned for her to sit next to me. She protested with a brief rehearsal of 'the details.'

"I only want a minute," I said. "The details will all take care of themselves for one minute."

She came and sat down by me. In that quiet moment we looked at the earth made fresh, clean, and renewed by the rain. We noticed the light steam of rising rejuvenation to the manicured flowers, bushes, and trees we had spent so much time preparing. I thought about this being my last moment as 'the Mom.' Not that I wouldn't still be her mother but from this day forward it would be different. It was sort of like my last legitimate command. She said later she was thinking it was her last moment to be just the daughter responding to the Mom. The air smelled like rain, like new, like a new life for both of us. It was reverent. We felt a spiritual presence; perhaps maybe God was placing His blessing and His mark on this forever after event. We felt like He was saying, "I am here. I approve. Be happy."

And then it was over. We stood up, we hugged each other, and the festivities proceeded dropping little memory sticks here and there. Some of us remembered one thing and others remembered something else. Of course we all remembered the photographer in the fountain. But for Rachel and I the three or four minutes of quiet solitude alone in the midst of all the chaos and important details of that day will stand out as a private sacred moment shared only between the two of us forever.

Finding your quiet mind can happen anywhere. It can be leaving your daily routine and surroundings and physically going someplace else, or it can be as simple as just stopping in the middle of whatever your life offers. Stop and become for one minute the observer. Breathe in the sights, sounds, smells, and ambience of the moment. Record it permanently into your mind's memory bank. Recall it at will whenever you feel stress, anger, or fear.

There are times when it is okay to retreat to the bathroom. Lock the door and let others think you are doing some important business. It's okay because 'this' is important business. Take a deep breath, shut your eyes, and block out the world.

You can find a quiet place, a quiet time, and a quiet mind. We give you permission to go there, to wear your soft soled shoes, and to rejuvenate your sole (soul).

Chapter 10 - What if I Walk Backwards, Turn Around 3 times, and Wear Purple Shoes?

Imagination versus Knowledge. Which is more important... knowledge or imagination?

Why do we care?

Life is challenging at best. If we understand what we know, why we know it, and how we know it, then faced with insurmountable challenges we will be able to access our own powers within.

Knowledge gives us power and security. Imagination gives us solutions to our problems and a sense of wonder. And then the patterns in our lives give us the stability to more effectively function both knowledge and imagination.

Do you always drive the same route to your regular known destinations?

We are all creatures of habit. If you don't believe that fact, step out of yourself for one week or even one day. Observe how may repetitive rituals or patterns you engage yourself in during your daily activities.

For example:

When and how do you get up in the morning and/or go to bed at night?

Notice how and when you brush your teeth, comb your hair, take medicine, or dress yourself.

How do you prepare your food? What do you eat, how do you eat it, and when or what time of the day do you eat different kinds of food? Are there things you would never eat for breakfast and other things you would never eat for dinner or just before going to bed?

What are your driving and/or walking routes or habits that get you from point A to point B?

Are there any exercise or personal behavior rituals or patterns in your daily routines?

What about television, cell phone, iPad, or other media habits?

Do you have any specific shopping routines?

What about children, spouse, and pet interactions?

Are there certain things you do repeatedly in your house and yard maintenance?

What about your religious practices?

What about any other avenues of your regular behaviors or routines?

Repetitions, routines, and rituals are soothing security blankets in our lives. They make us feel like we have control. With them we are stable and anchored. There is an element of safety in all of this. It goes back a bit to the "Shoebox" idea of Chapter 6.

Janie:

When this concept of daily rituals was presented to me I thought... not me. I won't be labeled as relying on some ritual to keep me grounded. This is stupid. I refuse to put my shoes and socks on my feet exactly the same way every day. I will not be that predictable.

Each time I discovered I was in a pattern or ritual mode, I changed my behavior. If I found I always put on my left sock and then my right sock, I reversed the order. I put on one sock and then one shoe and vice versa. I continued to alter any patterns or rituals in my daily routine.

Within a week my whole psyche was upset. I was snappy with everybody. Anything anybody did annoyed me almost to the point of screaming. My productivity practically disintegrated. At last I succumbed to the notion that maybe I needed rituals in my life.

They keep us grounded. They give us self-confidence. We feel a sense of control that allows us to be more tolerant of the things we have no control over.

I actually felt a sense of relief the next morning when I finally allowed myself to get out of bed, brush my teeth, and dress myself in my old quirky routine. The muscles in my neck released. I felt something warm flowing through my body. It was as though my circulation had been dammed up and today I opened the headgate. This day the unsettling problems of the previous day melted as bits of nothing. I was stunned at the way my brain capacity seemed so much greater today than it had the day before.

In retrospect it seemed to me that when I was in a pattern or ritual mode it gave my brain a chance to rest. I didn't have to think. My body went into automatic pilot. I think this resting period gave my brain a short moment to recharge before tackling the next crisis.

The patterns in our lives are important. We are all a bit OCD (obsessive compulsive disorder). If you are way over the top in this area perhaps you could get professional help. However, for most of us, the patterns of our repetitive behaviors are important to our mental health.

What we know and what we know how to do enables us. It gives us power. Knowledge is power. The more you know the more powerful you feel.

Yearn to learn. We must develop the sponge attitude and soak up every tidbit of knowledge we can.

Too many people think the only way to learn is to go to school or take some kind of class or course.

True, this is an important way of gaining knowledge. It is a very good way, a very desirable way, but it is not the only way.

Reading newspapers, magazines, searching online, watching information based television programs, talking to people, frequenting the public libraries, accessing all kinds of information systems, reading books, traipsing through museums, and the good old standby method of trial and error are also effective means of acquiring knowledge.

Learning broadens your vision and increases your opportunities. Gaining knowledge is and should be a rewarding adventure. It is very very important.

Knowledge is too important to be minimized in any way. That's why we have given it such a lengthy introduction here. You must understand how very important knowledge is in order to truly understand the magnitude of our next concept.

Albert Einstein stated. " Imagination is more important than knowledge."

Everybody has an imagination. Children, especially young children are masters at using their imaginations. They use their imagination because they don't have enough real life experiences yet to know the facts. Sometimes this is good and sometimes it is not. Your imagination never dies. Some adults do allow it to go dormant. They think using imagination is childish or silly. This is not true.

Knowledge is a compilation of facts somebody else discovered. If we know exactly what to do…it isn't a problem, it's a job. We may not want to do the job, but if we know what to do then the problem is not in finding a solution it is in summoning the fortitude to take care of the situation.

When we don't know what to do, when we have no solution to the problem, we call upon our imagination. We have no idea or knowledge of what to do, so the imagination mode of our brain just as when each one of us was a child has to kick in.

It is in our creative thinking that we solve the dilemmas confronting us. ***Our imagination is where we discover the solutions to our problems.***

Janie:

My husband is a paradox. His brain operates in numbers. His whole family has special gifts when it comes to mathematical problem solving. He remembers prices, measurements, and statistics religiously. He is a dyed in the wool facts man, strictly the facts. His knowledge of facts is astounding.

However, if I ever say, "I can't."

He says, "You can, you just choose not to."

Then he says, "There is always a way. The true question is... are you willing to pay the price? You just have to decide if the price is worth it."

When my husband switches to his 'anything is possible' mode his imagination as to how to accomplish something supersedes his knowledge, or in other words, his 'strictly the facts' attitude.

This little conversation of paying the price used to infuriate me. And then over time I watched 'The Master' in action. He has always been the epitome of the impossible. He has never been unemployed... he is between jobs. He is never broke... he is just temporarily out of cash. Nothing has ever been impossible in his mind.

As our children were growing up our family did some kind of an activity together once a week. On Sunday night we all sat together and discussed what that activity would be. I will never forget one particular Sunday. We were living in the 'old house.' Our financial situation was tight, belt tightening plate scraping tight.

"Any suggestions as to what we should do this week for our weekly activity?" my husband asked the kids.

My oldest daughter, Rachel, spoke up. She said there was an event she had heard about in San Diego. She really wanted the entire family to see it. "I think we should go there for our activity this week," she said. (Did I mention that we lived in Utah at the time?)

I took a deep breath and mentally prepared my "we can't afford to do things like that" speech.

My husband looked at Rachel and said, "That sounds like a great idea. How do you suggest we do it?"

The family has always harbored some version of a mexican plaster penny bank like the ones they sell from car to car as you are driving across the border out of Tijuana. The kids keep their change in this bank. Some of the banks were pigs, however, most of these banks have been in the shape of a huge multi-level hamburger. When a family vacation comes up we break open the bank, count the money and divide it by the number of children. This is their spending money for that particular trip. The more they have saved, the more they have to spend.

Rachel did in fact have a plan. It was a kid plan including of all kinds of possibilities and it sounded like the way kids plan things when they don't really have a handle on 'the facts.' As Rachel talked the other kids enthusiastically began throwing out ideas as well.

Of course this was all ludicrous. How long was my husband willing to let this discussion go before he gave them 'the facts.' We could hardly afford food, let alone take the whole family to San Diego.

The kids ended their brainstorming by asking to see how much money they had in 'the hamburger.' My husband called for the bank to be brought to him.

At this point I retired to the bedroom and called him to 'come here for a minute.'

"What are you doing? I demanded. "You know we can't afford to do this. Why are you letting the kids get their hopes up? I cannot let you do this to them. If you break that bank they will think we are really going to go."

"So maybe we are. Why are you being so negative?" He said.

"I am being realistic," I said, "look at the facts."

"Why don't you listen to their ideas? Stop looking at what you think reality is. They have some really creative suggestions as to how we could actually pull this off. I am willing to let them try to work out the details," he said,. Then he turned his back to me and walked back into the living room where the kids waited for him to break the bank.

My insides roiled. I thought I was going to be sick. I was convinced when the crushing blow came the children would be scarred for life and I would be the one who had to pick up the pieces and make it be all right again.

The plans kept taking on life. On Wednesday after school the kids' preparations came to fruition and we left for San Diego. A neighbor had loaned us his motorhome. We filled it with food we already had. We made homemade cookies and sandwiches with homemade bread to eat along the way. My husband called a dear friend of his who allowed us to park in his driveway while we were in California.

We drove straight through to the event Rachel wanted us to see in San Diego, and then spent one day going to Disneyland, and drove home. The kids only missed two days of school. Robert worked late the first half of the week at his job so he would not be missed for the two days we were away.

We still struggled along with our bills, but nothing was the worse for our having gone. And to this day the kids talk about the miracle of how it all worked out. Through the imaginations of the children we did the impossible.

I have even had some of my children who are now married say to me. "When I am faced with a situation that appears to be impossible I remember how impossible it was for us to go on that trip to San Diego. It reminds me that somehow there is always a way."

> **Einstein also said, "I think and think for months and years, ninety-nine times, the conclusion is false. The hundredth time I am right."**

True scientists understand the concept of imagination and creative thinking. This is how they come up with unproven theories and ideas of how things happen, or can happen. They then set out to prove or disprove this creative idea of someone's imagination into a factual knowledge based avenue. Knowledge and imagination can and should work hand in hand.

Every great discovery, concept, idea, or invention was a product of someone's imagination long before it ever became somebody's reality.

Creativity is a unique commodity. It cannot be bought.

Years ago several large companies offered their employees large sums of bonus money to come up with some totally new viable idea before the deadline of an up coming convention. The project failed. Why? Because creativity cannot be enticed with a bribe. It cannot be bought. It can be cultivated, nurtured and encouraged, but not forced. So offering a person an incentive such as money oftentimes frustrates our creativity more than enhancing it.

It is a bit like trying to force yourself to remember somebody's name or some fact you need to recall. The harder you try, the more blank your mind goes. It is when you relax and allow the information to flow at a slower pace that you remember with ease the information that you stressed over previously.

So the end of the story was that after the convention was over and the incentive was gone someone in each of the three companies did come up with an idea that proved unique, innovative, and profitable for each different company. The results sent each company in a different but not more or less important direction of their industry.

One of the problems with our current society is called the 'thirty-minute sitcom solution.' We put time limits on all aspects of our life.

We want all our problems to be solved in thirty minutes. If they are not we think we are doomed for the rest of our lives.

We have all kinds of deadlines that must be met. It begins with school. Every project must be completed before the end of the term. The problem with this deadline mentality is that it fosters a conflict with quality work or a value or lack of value on how long it takes to complete a project. This mentality carries over into the work field as well.

Janie:

My oldest son was a straight A student. In Junior High School he had a beginner shop class. I received notice at midterm that he was failing the class. When I questioned him about it he had no idea why. He said he had been working on his project diligently and had never gotten in any kind of trouble.

"What is the problem here?" I asked his teacher.

"Well," the teacher said, "you see, the kids have to hand in projects to get points for their grade and your son, Richard, has not handed in any projects, so he hasn't got any points."

I turned to Richard. "How come you haven't turned in any projects?"

"Because I am making a lazy-susan turnstyle to sit on our table." He then walked over to his project to show it to me. It was a large wooden circle with a tiny wooden fence around the edge. It rotated on a rolling base. Richard had about 1/3 of the tiny fence left to make and then he had to stain the whole piece and then it would be finished.

I was surprised at the amount of work this project appeared to require. "Is this a beginner project?" I asked the teacher.

"Not really," the teacher said, "but I let the kids choose their own projects and this is what he wanted to make. The problem is that the class is mandated on a point system and I can't give any points until he hands in finished work. Even if he finishes this project it won't give him enough points to pass the class."

"So what can he do?" I asked.

"He can make some of the things the rest of the class is making," said the teacher. He showed me squares of plastic. The kids heated the sides and pushed them upward slightly. He called these candy dishes. Cutting those same squares in half or in fourths and drilling a hole in the corner, and adding a chain, they are called key chains.

Richard finished his lazy-susan and spent the rest of the term making key chains and candy dishes to get his point score up to an A grade. He felt he was wasting his time and never chose to take another shop class. My house was filled with square plastic pieces that had the sides pushed up and brightly colored squares of plastic with chains through the holes. We gave them away to anybody who took the time to ask us what they were?

I am not really faulting the school system here. There are many variables of this problem at work. What I am saying is that because we are so deadline oriented we fail to foster creativity. Hence by the time we have finished with the education process and moved into the working world most of us have had to bury our imaginations and creativity for the sake of day-to-day requirements.

How do you keep your imagination from being squelched by societal norms?

How do you tap into the power source of your imagination?

First you have to find ways to keep it active and alert. It is that darn exercise clause. The more you exercise your physical body, the more physically fit, healthy, and active you become. The same holds true for your mind.

Start with small things. If you always come home from work/school/the gym the same way try altering your course. Take a road you never take and see where it goes. Try making or eating something completely different than your normal eating habits and/or routine.

Janie:

I was looking for an address in a small town. I stopped and asked a person standing on the street if they were local. "Yep, I have lived here all my life," was the reply. I was so happy to find somebody who could help me. I explained where I needed to be and asked if I turned down 'this' road... would I arrive at my destination. "I have no idea," said the person. "I don't believe I have ever gone down that road before."

It was a small town with maybe only ten or twenty roads or streets in the town central. This person had lived in this town his whole life and he had never ventured down that road before... how sad is that?

Drive down the roads of your town/city and see where they go and what they have to offer.

Change your hairstyle.

Wear something different.

Rearrange the furniture.

Try cloud watching. What do the shapes look like to you? What do they make you think about?

Play with a child. Listen to the child use his or her imagination.

Just for fun try this exercise with your spouse or partner; "If money was no object... I would?" or "If I could do anything I really wanted I would....?" or "If I could go anyplace it would be....... and why... or what I would do when I got there?" or If I won the Publisher's Clearing House..... I would?" Remember the rules.... The other person can say anything.... It doesn't matter, this is all pretend... Don't get offended, no matter what is said. Allow each person imaginative latitude. You are not locking anybody into any kind of commitment. This is an activity where you believe "The Sky is the Limit." Have fun!

Mark Twain said, "I only open my mail once a month. By then most problems have taken care of themselves."

The next time you are faced with a problem:

First relax.

Let your patterns and daily rituals re-establish your confidence and control.

Review what you know

What is your real knowledge of the problem? What are the facts?

Perhaps make a list of real information.

Then stop focusing on the obvious facts.

Step out of the picture and try to see the issue from an unbiased observation.

Let your imagination take over.

Think of every absurd solution you can conjure up.

Allow yourself time. Unless your house is on fire or your family is in immediate danger of destruction, you do not have to have the answer right this minute. Give yourself the time to consider your options.

Following this process you might actually come up with a fresh approach to the situation you hadn't thought of before.

Try walking backwards, turning around three times and wear purple shoes.... You never know it might help. It surely couldn't hurt.

Chapter 11 - I Dare You to Wear that Pair of Shoes.

I double-dog-dare you to wear those shoes!

Do you remember those days as a kid? Maybe you never had to face the neighborhood bully. Maybe you never had friends who wanted you to be the fall guy before they tried something dangerous or stupid. Maybe you were the bully or the kid who was afraid to try until you saw how the other kid faired.

It is all a question of courage.

As a kid the pressure seemed to come from others. As a person gets older she looks elsewhere to lay the blame. "The Devil made me do it."

The truth is… you decide. In every instance… you decide. Now that decision may be greatly influenced by the consequences. Often the consequences are choosing something bad or choosing something worse, but the ultimate decision is always yours. This particular topic is discussed in greater detail elsewhere in this book. What we want to focus on here is that all decisions take courage. It takes courage to act.

In this day of texting, blogging, and other media communication devices, people are hiding. Meaningful relationships are suffering. It is so much easier to say things when the person is not standing right next to you. It is so simple. If you don't like what is happening or what is being said you can 'log out,' 'shut off,' or 'delete.'

Stepping out of your comfort zone and serving somebody in real life, in real time, investing in a friendship face-to-face, or trying something completely unrelated to your normal safety net, is dangerous.

You could face rejection, criticism, or failure.... Oh my!

Think of Dorothy from the Wizard of Oz. She had to trust a scarecrow, a tin man, and a lion to help her get back home. By the end of the story this unusual foursome had forged a binding friendship.

Friends are found in the strangest places and in the strangest ways. A real friendship takes time. It takes sacrifice. It takes risk. It takes courage. It also takes love and a bit of blindness. In the end a true friendship brings us a little closer to God. In the end it might be that friendship, the one you have invested in deeply, that saves your sole (soul).

Where do you find this kind of friend? Some of them are leftovers from childhood.

Kids have all kinds of other kids attached to them. Some come from school, some from sports, some from other kinds of activities, but most are deemed to be friends of one kind or another. As the years go by these friends begin to drop off like those trying to sit on the spinning plate in the amusement park. The ones remaining are the ones who, for whatever reason, lock arms around the center of that spinning platform refusing to allow those they have connected with to be thrown into the fray.

Lyn:

The Slumber party

It was a slumber party for fifty-year-olds.

To Patti, Julie & Jean:

Your laughter has been the soundtrack to many of my life's favorite memories.

A short time ago I went to a slumber party with my three best friends from Junior High. We try to celebrate our friendship by taking a weekend holiday once a year. We live in different states (and sometimes I am even in a different country) and we don't see each other very often, but the bond we created so many years ago has glued us together for life.

This particular year we made reservations at a motel in a town where no one knew us. We planned our trip months in advance so we could each stash away enough money to do some serious shopping if we found something worth buying. And our early planning gave us something to look forward to throughout the dreary winter months.

By now, most of our children had left the nest and the few that are left are old enough to fend for themselves, so that was not a problem. However, since this is an annual event, in earlier years we left them with their fathers or other reliable babysitters. It is good for children to have a few days away from mom once in awhile. It is especially good for husbands. Everyone needs to feel loved and appreciated and nothing makes you appreciate a mother more than her absence for a couple of days.

Ten minutes on the road and we were giggling and confiding in each other. We even flirted with unsuspecting truck drivers just like we used to when we were eighteen. There is a special bond between old friends that nothing or no one can replace.

We can go for months without seeing each other and yet when we get back together, there is no uncomfortable getting reacquainted again routine. There is no catching up to do. I know these friends will never act shocked at anything I tell them. Once in awhile we are shocked, but we have learned to listen before we start throwing out the questions. I can always be honest about my feelings and they never condemn or judge me. We can tell each other our wildest fantasies and darkest fears, and when we are finished we know it will never go further than the confines of the car.

We had the time of our lives, eating good food, giggling, reminiscing, bragging, (mostly about our grandbabies) and sometimes even crying. All four of us had lived through some very hellish times in our half of a century and we had been there for each other through all of them. There had been so many changes in our lives since "the good old days." Trials and challenges seem more bearable when you can talk about them. Saying it out loud in a safe place somehow deflates the problem elephant in the room. Poof... it reduces to nothing but a silly cartoon. It might inflate again later, but for now it can be minimized by poking fun at it. And if it does inflate later the memory of that laughter makes it never quite so large or ominous.

We wondered out loud how our lives would have been different if we had made different choices. We sifted and sorted, and analyzed scenarios from our past. We discussed the men in our lives that we did not marry and how our lives would have been different if we had. And we also speak of the ones we did marry and how our lives might have been if we hadn't.

We whispered deep into the night and laughed until our faces ached. I know their faults and weaknesses and they know mine, but we love each other unconditionally. There are also times when words are not even necessary. We are not all alike in our dreams, goals, or beliefs. We have very different personalities, tastes, and habits. It is extremely valuable to appreciate our differences and learn from them. Over the years some of the most profound lessons I have learned have been from my friends.

I met Patti in the seventh grade when she stole my boyfriend from me. Many boys have come and gone since then, but my friendship with Patti will last forever. Because of how this works, many years ago my husband and I realized and tried to tell our children that it wasn't important for them to be popular. We felt that if they could find one or two good friends, whom they could enjoy, who hopefully harbored high standards, that was all that mattered.

Mark Twain wrote. "To get the full value of joy you must have someone to divide it with."

Isn't that true? What is the first thing you want to do when something good happens to you? You want to share it with a friend.

Life is too short to spend it alone or even within the confines of your own family. A true friend is your lifeline to sanity. When you sincerely love your friends you see the beauty in their souls. Their goodness is evident no matter what their outer appearance may be. And you are proud of them.

Lyn:

I feel no jealousy toward my dearest friends. Their accomplishments, talents, and blessings are mine as well.

Does a true friendship have to begin in childhood to make it lasting? Absolutely not. Some of the very best friends--the kindred spirits--are people who have met in later years. You can be drawn to each other with like interests, similar tragedies, or common viewpoints. It may even be something as simple as a game of Mah Jong. True friendships have no age barriers.

Lyn:

One of my dearest friends is close to my mother's age and another is ninety. I am also very close to many younger people. I would do anything for these friends and I believe they would for me. One time when I had been very ill for several months, my friend, Sudy, shaved my legs and cut my toenails! I like to say that a friend is one who will bring you a meal or flowers when you are sick, but a "true friend" will clean your toilet.

If I had the power to grant you one wish, it would be that each of you could have a true friend.

We remind you once again. "To have a friend you must be a friend."

Don't wait for the other person to call you or do you a kindness. Begin today to be the best friend you can be and you will be amazed at the shape your life will take.

Where are friends found? Answer: everywhere you look.

Janie:

A friend of mine recounted this experience:

It was a day of tending kids who were similar ages to my own children when I realized I had to run an important errand that could not wait. I loaded all the kids into my car and set off. The kids were rowdy, complaining and poking at each other. I came to an intersection and the light turned red.

I turned around to take care of the chaos behind me. Suddenly I became aware that the light must have changed to green and then back to red while I was dealing with the kid misconduct in the back seat.

I looked up to see if there were any vehicles behind me. There was one car. I could clearly see the face of a gray haired man. He smiled and waved to me. I gratefully smiled and waved back. I made an "I am so sorry" gesture with my face and hands. He gave me a thumbs-up.

That man will be my friend forever.

It takes courage to serve others. Serving others is the lifeblood of peace. It takes courage to change. It takes courage to believe. It takes courage to act.

It takes courage to succeed. The easy way out is to settle on being a scrub.

You can blame all your failings on past circumstances. Your father beat you. You took drugs. Your mother was verbally abusive. You were sexually abused. Your parents were divorced. You have asthma. You were a sickly child. You have some kind of handicap. You moved around a lot. You never did well in school, yada, yada, yada, yada. Whatever it was it was your worst nightmare. It affected the way you act, talk, think, and behave. It was terrible, but… it is past and you cannot change that circumstance no matter how hard you try. Nothing you do will ever change your past. Wishing with all your heart will not change your past. Rehashing it over and over and over will not change one bit of your past. Why? Because it is past.

Why will you let some horrible yesterday rob you of all of your precious tomorrows? It takes courage to let it go. The reason it takes courage to let it go is because if you let it go then you will have to take responsibility for your failures today. When you let it go you can no longer use your past as your excuse for lackluster performance or not reaching whatever that level of perfection is. Horrors… you might actually fail, legitimately fail!

Failing does not condemn you to be a failure. Failing simply shows you what you don't want to do next time. It is the questions on the test you miss that you remember the most.

It is the mistakes that give you the experiences that change your life.

You never see new parents encouraging their toddler baby to walk, and when the baby topples over, they run to the child, pick it up and say, "Oh you poor child. We don't want you to get hurt. We don't want you to experience failure, so, we are never going to let you try to walk, ever again.

What happens is the mom or the dad picks the baby up, sets her on her feet and starts coaxing the child to try again. Fall down, get up. Fall down, get up. Fall down, get up. She bangs her head. She cries. Still the parents stand her up and encourage her to try again. Until at last the child has developed the muscles strong enough to sustain that growing body. She has learned how to use her arms for balance. She trusts her parents. She lets go of the chair, focuses on Dad's outstretched arms and walks. Everybody cheers.

Why can't we cheer others on to succeed like we do babies trying to walk and talk?

For some odd reason, most adults cheer older children and other adults on to fail. It is so much harder for any of us to succeed when the rhetoric sounds like this, "I knew that business would fail." "What was she thinking?" "I can't believe she tried that."

Janie:

When one of our children started making life choices that we did not agree with our hearts were broken. We were angry. We were disappointed. We were afraid. What had we done wrong?

First we began blaming ourselves. When that didn't change anything we began blaming the surroundings. When that didn't help, we began condemning the child.

One day when we were particularly dismayed over what this child was doing. I heard my husband and I saying things like, "This kid is never going to succeed. No way will anything turn out the way this kid thinks it will."

I stopped. It was like I was watching a movie. What did I want the end of this story to be?

I said to my husband. "In the end when this child... our child, does fail are we going to wave banners as we stand on the sidelines watching, and shout, "Yeah... we knew we were right? Hooray.... The kid failed!"

Immediately we changed our tactics. We began to cheer the child on to succeed. Whenever there was anything we could say encouraging, we did. Eventually the child came to make better choices and told us in later years that many of those course correcting decisions were based on the fact that this child... our child, knew of our love and support. We did not condone nor accept the bad behavior but our love and support for our child was never again in question.

It takes courage to succeed. In order to succeed you must, at some point, step into the dark forest of the unknown, the forest of fear. If you don't believe this, go watch the movie, Snow White, again.

That evil witch stepmother queen who was bent on the destruction of the poor young Snow White actually gave her the key to happiness. Such is the case with most of the adversities in people's lives.

When Snow White finally found the courage to make it through the forest of fear, she was then able to have a grand adventure. She learned many things from all of those little dwarf men and in the end she married the handsome prince and lived happily ever after.

If the evil stepmother had been nice, Snow White would have missed the forest experience and what a shallow life that would have been. Not to mention the fact she would have missed her chance at a movie contract to be immortalized forever with fame and fortune.

Find your Passion and Strive for Excellence.

Such a compact tidy little phrase…find your passion and strive for excellence. How do you find your passion in the first place? And then when you do, how do you fit it in between dishes, laundry, work, and family?

First of all your passion will change with time. In one lifetime you may and should experience many passions. And that is the way it is supposed to be.

Janie:

In elementary school, Karen Sato drew pictures of horses. Her horses looked like photographs. I could not draw horses like Karen so I told myself I had no artistic ability even though deep in my heart I yearned to be an artist.

Years passed and I married, had a couple of kids and life happened. A lady moved into a house near me. It was a new house and I mustered my courage to visit the lady and welcome her into our neighborhood. She invited me inside and showed me around her beautiful home. It was tastefully decorated. I was impressed. That is until we walked into her formal dining room and there on the wall was the worst oil painting I had ever seen. It probably wasn't the worst oil painting I had ever seen, but it was the worst one I had ever seen hanging in such a prominent place, in such a nice house. The jarring effect of it stopped me like I had just stepped in dog doo-doo.

"What do you think of my picture?" The lady asked. "I painted it myself."

She continued. "I know," she said as she watched my face, "it is pretty bad isn't it?"

"Uhh," I said trying to recover the awkward moment. "Uhhh, I am just surprised to see it hanging in that spot." (Nice save, I thought.)

"Actually," the lady said, "I have always wanted to be an artist. I know I will never be a Rembrandt or anything like that, but everywhere we live I take an art class and then I hang my best work on the wall. When I complete my next class I take down the first picture and hang up the new one. I figure that way I can see the progress I am making. Who knows? Maybe one day I will actually be good at it."

I was stunned at the lady's courage. It is one thing to do something you know you are gifted in. It is quite another to attempt something you want to try whether you have any natural talent or not.

The example of that woman changed my life. It gave me permission to not be perfect and it is okay. I don't have to be born with natural talent and abilities to try something new. It is acceptable to do it simply for fun. And it is exhilarating.

Pound those keys on the piano. Somebody might even recognize that the tune is Silent Night. And then again maybe they won't. It does not matter what people say, or think. It does not matter if you are lousy at soccer, bowling, or tennis. The courage to try is reward enough. And it is a proven fact if you keep trying you will improve in whatever you do. If you enjoy the journey keep working at your chosen whatever. If you hate it? Life is too short to hang onto unnecessary baggage. Let it go and try something else.

"That which we persist in doing becomes easier. Not that the nature of the thing has changed, but that our ability to do it has increased." Ralph Waldo Emerson

The same thing is true on the flip side of things. If you practice being a grumpy negative person you will become a professional grumpy negative person.

If you walk up and down the aisles at the grocery store criticizing the way that lady wears her shorts too short, the other guy's hair is too long, or that person by the frozen food has way too much body hanging out, it never helps or improves any of the problems. And as a matter of fact who said they are problems? It is merely your perception of what a problem is that is making you critical of the situation.

The comment, "That lady has a heart attack to go, stacked in her cart," will never improve the lady's eating habits one iota. Neither will saying, "How can people buy so much of that kind of junk food stuff?"

The same is true on the home front. If your kids can never do anything to please you and you tell them this on a regular basis, where is the incentive to change? Why try? Their rooms are never clean enough. They have bad friends. They stay up too late. Your husband won't help around the house. There is never enough money, etc, etc, etc. With this attitude, nothing will ever improve.

Everybody can always find really juicy stuff to grump about. There is never a shortage of problems to complain over.

However, if you practice kindness, compassion, serving others, and listening, the rewards of perfecting those skills will far exceed anything negative. This is a proven law of nature. And the only way we can think of to explain how it works is to visualize a glass. If the glass is empty it is empty. It cannot be anymore empty than it already is. There is only so much empty and there cannot be anymore (you mathematicians out there don't start up on negative numbers here, I am talking about zero that can't be anymore or less than zero… once you go beyond zero in the negative stance you start having something again.).

But what constitutes full? If you take that same glass and fill it with scoops of ice cream, is the glass full? Take the glass and pour syrup in between the scoops of ice cream. Is it full now? Carefully pour sparkling water into the glass. When the water reaches the rim of the glass is it full now? Take an aerosol can of whipping cream and swirl a peak of whipped cream on top. Is the glass full now? Sprinkle on a few chopped nuts and then add a cherry. Is it full now? What about a straw?

Think about it. What actually constitutes a full or a fulfilling event in your life?

And now you better finish off that soda before all the ice cream melts.

One person may be perfectly happy to have the scoops of ice cream and skip all the rest. Another person may want only ice cream with whipped cream, nuts or no nuts, whatever. It is your passion. Take it as far as you need or want to go, and then let it go. Be grateful for the place it filled in your soul at this moment in time. Then move on.

Having courage to move on is just as important as the other aspects of courage, sometimes more so. If you had a bad past, you had it. Acknowledge it. Thank your past for all you have learned from it. Appreciate it. Then use it as a stepping-stone to greater heights. Leave the bad stuff behind. Take the lessons learned with you. Share what you have with others. Maybe your knowledge will help somebody else avoid your pitfalls.

Janie:

What about my painting lady friend? She invited me to take art classes with her and I did. She improved steadily. By the time I moved away the quality of her paintings were sellable. Mine were not, but I did my best. I improved with time. More importantly I was fulfilled.

The nature of most normal human beings is to be inwardly focused. Everybody has a dialog going on inside of his or her head all of the time, so the natural thing is to feel like your world revolves around your thoughts, what you want, what you need, what you don't have, what you did, what you want to do, etc.

It takes courage to step out of your head.

Now we don't want conflict with any mental health people here, but it goes back to the dual being concept we discussed earlier.

There is the 'yearning' you. This 'you' wants to try to paint, sing, dance, talk to the neighbors, be president of something, or you fill in the blank………..

And there also is the 'yah-but' you. Every time the yearning part of you has an idea the yah-but you says, "Yah, that's a good idea, but… you are no public speaker, you haven't any degree, you will be laughed at, nobody will listen to you, your ideas stink, etc. etc. etc.

This may be a surprise but both of these 'you's' are very important and very necessary. In writing the two are called 'the writer'" and the 'editor/critic.' It is important to have balance. After the writer writes, the editor hones, perfects, and throws out the junk. The same is true for the 'yearning you' and the 'yah-but you.' The yah-but you keeps you paying your bills and being responsible. The yearning you looks outward with a hopeful anticipation. The yearning you needs to be nurtured and encouraged, but not at the expense of reasonable balance.

Janie:

Reasonable balance recognizes that sometimes sacrifices are warranted in the name of your passion. For example: Right now I have laundry stacked up, unwashed dishes, and floors that need attention, but I am writing. Fortunately I have a supportive husband who puts up with my writing passion. He will almost always make dinner and sometimes he will even do other household chores. At some point, however, I know that I need to stop and get caught up on the 'life process,' reclaim my rightful responsibilities, and spend some time showing my husband and family my appreciation for the support they give to me.

What if you feel like they do not give you the support you want or need? Thank them anyway.

Be genuine. Find something even if it is small and let them know you appreciate your son who brought in the garbage cans from the street. Okay you told him three times to do it, but he finally did.... Celebrate it! Your husband gave you a peck on the cheek when he came home from work just before he planted himself into the couch like he was waiting to grow up again and the television was his plant food. Thank him for not harping about the carpet not being vacuumed and the newspapers strewn around the room from yesterday. The more gratitude you show, the more your family will try to please you.

If you keep some semblance of balance in your life then you will actually have more energy and time for your passions. When you are out of balance the guilt of things you should be doing can drain the impetus, enthusiasm, and creative flow from your passion.

Now when somebody dares you to "wear those shoes," you will confidently step forward and to the surprise of all, you will take the dare, or you will smile and walk away without so much as a backward glance.

Chapter 12 - So What if Your Shoes get Wet

Becoming attuned to the majesty of the world and what it offers renews our soles (souls) and energizes us.

Janie:

I was sulking. It was a dramatic change going from a life of more than plenty of money to our having lost it all and being broke. I felt trapped. I could not afford a babysitter. I could not go shopping, or do any of the things that had been part of my previous life. My husband had taken a job that required him to travel out of state, so I was also alone most of the time. We lost our big luxurious house and moved to a small farming community into a much smaller turn-of-the-century home that needed a lot of work. I did not have any of the household conveniences I had in the 'big house.' There was no dishwasher, convected oven, central vacuum system, or even a garbage disposal. We all had to share one bathroom for eight people. One of my sons slept on the floor because there was no bed for him and no place to put a bed even if we had one.

We had moved a long way from my friends and I did not have any family living close to me either. My life was hard. I did not want any of this. I felt like none of what I was resigned to deal with was my fault. I was sad. I was lonely. I was depressed.

What I wanted to do was run away but I had no place to go and no money to get there. Besides, if I left what would happen to my kids?

I walked outside. Our backyard was open to a twenty-acre farm. I stood watching the farmer preparing the soil to plant this year's crops. It was familiar. I had grown up in a farming family. Beyond the farm I had a view of The Great Salt Lake. Even though the sun was shinning there was still a slight chill tempering this early spring day. For a long time I remained motionless. The air prickled my skin. My body was drinking in the freshness of the season. The earth and its forces were healing me but I was oblivious to the source of my renewal.

I was determined, however, to be depressed, so I threw my frumpy attitude along with my body onto the ground and positioned my head face down on my forearms staring into the grass. I tried to force the tears. I wanted to cry. I deserved to be miserable and I was going to be miserable in spite of myself.

I rehearsed in my brain all the reasons I had for this private pity party. Try as I might I could not seem to conjure up any tears. Instead of crying I was distracted by all the little bugs busily going about their business amongst the grasses and dirt. I became philosophically interested in their existence and their lack of concern for my childish behavior.

I became so interested watching them I forgot all about forcing myself to 'suffer' because my lifestyle had changed.

When I finally stood up I felt like I had been on a mini vacation, a short respite from all my problems. Rewinding my thoughts I remembered, "Oh yes, I am supposed to be angry, upset and depressed." I was surprised by how long I had been entertained by this little bug civilization.

Although I had always appreciated nature and its inherent benefits this was the first time I recognized its dramatic therapeutic properties. Over the next few days I marveled as I returned to my bug observation spots. I felt energy emerging from the ground. It penetrated my body. I can't really explain exactly what it was. The dynamics of a surging power regenerated the batteries of my physical self and brain. As I sat on the grass it invigorated me.

I began having picnics in the backyard with the children and showing them the bug world in the grass. We talked about whether or not the bugs watched us. We made up stories guessing what they might be thinking of us. This was long before the animated movies about humanized bugs found place at the box office. We also spent time examining the different bark patterns on the different kinds of trees. I even climbed the big poplar tree along with the kids. A sense of personality and life emitted from things in the yard I had taken for granted as nothing more than part of the scenery.

A Great Horned Owl dropped into one of our trees and parked himself there. He was huge. The children called all their friends to come over to see the phenomenon. The owl stayed for several days. I began to wonder if there was something wrong with it and called the Forestry Service. They told me to call them back if the owl was still there a week later. Every day we had our owl update report from the kids checking to see if he was still perched on his branch. The day before I was to call the Forestry guys again he was gone. This was the largest bird any of us had ever seen. We were kind of sad when he left.

The kids made teepee tents out of sheets and our simple yard transformed into everything from the Old West to an Alien Planet. Along with bugs and birds, this yard accommodated cats, mice, snakes, dogs, chickens and pigs. It was a vacation from the rat race of the world. We even saw a few rats here and there.

Alone with the kids, I grew to appreciate the rejuvenating powers found in a small patch of dirt, a little grass, and a few trees.

Not one of the women in our survey denied the impact of nature on their personal welfare. It seems that being out amongst living things, sunlight and clean air, are essential to good health. We are rejuvenated after a brisk walk, or taking in the fragrance of a bloom. Try stepping into a spring morning after a rain, notice how fresh and pure the air is and how vibrant the colors are. Fill your lungs with the scent of a flower. Our bodies crave these sensations. They are hints of heaven.

We need to be outdoors, to study a tree, sit on a rock, dip our toes into an icy river, or dig into the deep rich soil of a garden.

Lyn:

When you are having a bad day, go outside. Your body is actually craving sunlight and movement. One winter while living in Utah we had a long bout of fog. It was so dense and thick that schools and stores were closed. We literally could not see past the front porch of our home. As the days turned to weeks, people started going stir-crazy. We actually heard on the news of people who had committed suicide. Doctors were speaking on television and radio stations and telling people to go to the mountains even though it was the dead of winter. I remember one doctor saying, "Take your family and a picnic and go to a ski-resort and even if you don't ski sit there for the day. There, the sun is still shining above this heavy layer of fog and you will be hopeful that there will be a brighter, clearer day soon. Let the sun heal you from the outside in."

I have thought of these words often over the years during bouts of sorrow and regret as well as physical illness.

I love to see people at the park or camping. The next time you pass by notice how happy these people are. They are happy because they have made time for themselves and their loved ones. They are enjoying nature and their journey.

What amazed us most about this question in the survey was the transformation that came over each woman's face when asked the question about the effects of nature. The lines disappeared. The corners of each mouth relaxed. A sweet youthful twinkle filled their eyes. With simply the thought of nature their breathing slowed. If thought alone can do so much, what might you look like after spending an hour in your special place?

My favorite place in the whole world is lying in my hammock in my yard in Idaho. I love to read there, and look at the lush trees above me. And best of all I love to cuddle up to my grandchildren and sing with them. When my grandkids are visiting they are my number one priority, I simply stop all work and enjoy them and the glorious nature that surrounds us at River's Edge. But when they are not there and I am working, I push myself so hard that my body finally yells, "Stop!" I don't know why I do this to myself. No one is telling me it must be done by a certain time. My husband doesn't pressure me, but I still find myself self-imposing a strict workload.

Last spring I walked under the trees where my hammock was supposed to hang and I suddenly realized that I had been so busy I had forgotten to hang the hammock and enjoy the yard. Six weeks of fine weather had slipped by me and I had never once taken the time to lie in my favorite place and relax.

I am a list maker and I like to see at the beginning of my day what I need to accomplish. I went straight to my planner and I wrote "one hour hammock time" into my schedule. Then I worked harder dreaming of my hour in the hammock, which I remembered to appreciate every day after that and what a joy those hours were!

In my garden I have a rock with this saying carved into it, "In my garden the answers come." I truly believe that God sends messages through the earth and flowers. My big country garden is a lot like me; old-fashioned yet modern, brilliant and faded, tangy and sweet, thistly and tender and always abundant and colorful. I go there and begin to pull weeds and soon I find myself in fervent prayer about something or someone. I ask questions, I plead, I affirm, sometimes I rant and rave. And then I quiet my mind and pull more weeds listening intently to the answers Heaven brings me. Sometimes I argue with the answer and ask for a different one, but I always concede. In the end my heart and head turn the issue over to God like a child blowing dandelion seeds across a field. I hand it over to Him knowing that His way is always better than anything I could imagine.

When you have emptied your soul's power, go out into nature and if that is not possible bring a piece of nature into your home. Janie and

I both do this; we are two little scavengers, we are little girls at heart. If you watched the two of us at the beach or on a mountain you would think we were six years old. We love rocks and seashells and bits of sea glass and crystals, pressed wildflowers and pieces of wood.

Another way to feel better is to wear bright colors, hang some sunshine on your weary shoulders. Spend time looking at beautiful paintings and art, even photos of flowers and landscapes can heal. Listening to beautiful music or the simple songs of nature also soothe a drained spirit. These small favors to yourself reach into your soul. You can actually paint yourself well, with a wash of brilliant color and love. Paint yourself a new outlook and you will receive a positive outcome. Let God's light reach your soul. Let Him paint you happy.

If you don't believe God loves you…Step into nature.

Go ahead Try It!

Lyn:

What about water? I have always been drawn to water. I was born on the cusp of Aquarius and Pisces, so maybe that has something to do with it. When I was a child some of my fondest memories are of camping trips. Our tiny homemade camper and truck were pulled next to the Logan River or a smaller tributary. It did not matter to me if the water was big or small, a lake or a river--if the spot had water I wanted to be there. I would slip on my old worn out tennis shoes, choose a sturdy stick and wade off to be Sacajawea leading Lewis and Clark to the Pacific. I could sit for hours by a river. On those banks I would read and retain what I was reading better than anyplace on earth.

I was in the seventh grade before I saw the ocean for the first time. I was so awestruck I could not speak. It affects me still the same way even now. The day I sat in the sand on the edge of the Atlantic, I felt its pull every bit as much as the first time I saw it.

I have always longed to live near water and a few years ago my wish came true at River's Edge in Idaho. Butch found me a home on the

Snake River, the actual river Sacajawea had trail blazed! River's Edge has become a sanctuary of sorts for friends and family and an occasional retreat for writers, healers, and artists. It is a place for anyone who needs time to rejuvenate and rest from his or her trials. It is a special place, not because we live there. We really have little to do with the spiritual energy that encircles the grounds and the river and ponds, but we love and cherish it. We both know how blessed we are to have been given the privilege of being its caretakers for a time.

River's Edge is nature at her finest--flowers of many varieties, several types of trees including pines, poplars, fruit trees and Aspens, a pond full of colorful fat trout, rocks, grass, and raspberries galore. Animals of all shapes and sizes, ducks, eagles, osprey, moose, deer, raccoons, beaver and others birds of song and festive colors grace us with the presence of their comings and goings. And then there is the water which is a life unto itself, ever constant--ever changing. Just sitting on the deck and hearing her melody heals.

Recently I found myself sitting on the edge of North Africa, on the Atlantic Ocean in Agadir, Morocco. Remember my story about the scrapbook? This scene...where I was sitting right at that moment was a picture in that book! When I made my scrapbook I just cut and pasted. I did not put any restrictions in my mind on how or when. At the time I made the book I didn't even know there was such a place as Agadir, Morocco, let alone where it was. I had no clue this idea thing worked that way. I leave those details to a higher power.

When I first arrived there I was ill and as the weeks progressed my illness worsened. I lost twenty-seven pounds in two months and my chest felt like a car was parked on it. I was dizzy and nauseated all the time and my vision and focus were impaired. I finally became so weak that I knew something was seriously wrong. I called my doctor in America and he confirmed what I already knew in my heart. He said, "You need to come home, Lyn, right now."

I was so scared. My family had a history of heart disease, diabetes, and cancer. My only hope was that whatever was wrong was at least treatable. I hated the thought of going home alone--dreaded the thirty hours on planes and in airports. I worried about staying alone at home while the doctors sorted the puzzle pieces of my illness.

I had two days left in Morocco before my flight back to Idaho. I felt inspired and urged to spend those last two days outside. I felt drawn to the beach. The soft sand felt so warm on my feet. I walked slowly along the shore and let the waves push and pull me in and out. I prayed that the doctors could find answers, and that I would be strong enough to bear those answers, and then do whatever it took to become well.

I turned my face into the sun, lifted my weak and shaking arms out from my sides as if giving myself to God and the water. Suddenly a thought exploded in my head like the waves crashing against the distant rocks. The message, or command I heard in my head said, "Go, Lyn, go deep into the water. You are asking for help and we say, immerse yourself, let these ancient waters heal and protect you. Get Wet!"

I began shaking all over now. I was too weak and dizzy to go for a swim. Nevertheless I began to walk into the sea. It rose to my calves and then to my thighs and waist. Many times I had to stop and steady myself or wait for a blackout to subside. The North Atlantic isn't exactly balmy in November. My teeth began to chatter. I almost turned back. This was ludicrous, I was so sick. This was insane. I stood as still as the sea would allow but she was in full charge now.

And then I heard a soft female voice murmur over the rolling surf, "Don't be afraid, let me cover your heart."

And before I had time to make a decision the ocean decided for me... A wave three times as high as the last one wiped my legs out from under me. After struggling for a few seconds, I found my footing and stood. I welcomed wave after glorious wave as they strengthened and blessed me. When I stepped from the water I knew that whatever was wrong and whatever I had to endure, I would not be doing it alone.

(Note: Lyn's condition was a combination of several things including a severe inner ear infection and a dangerous life threatening depletion of Vitamin B-12. With supplements and a healthier diet she has made a complete recovery.)

What does it mean to be one with the universe?

All of the elements found in our physical bodies are found everywhere on this earth from the water in the rivers to the rocks in the road. When scientists break down the molecular structure of anything they find that the same elements are found in all of it. This eventually breaks down to atoms, neutrons and protons, etc. We are the earth and the earth is us, in the literal sense of the word.

And what of the mystical properties of water? Therapists have discovered various ways water and the sound of water soothes the mind. That is why fountains of every variety, especially desktop versions have become so popular in recent years.

Take a minute if you get the chance to sit near a waterfall, creek, river, or lake. Observe how your physical body reacts. Generally there is a relaxing or letting go effect. The muscles in your neck and across the shoulders will release. Stress will drain. For some there is a sort of hypnotic aspect.

The scientific experimentation of a man named Masaru Emoto is worth investigating. He established a way to photograph water crystals. He then exposed water to various kinds of stimuli and photographed the water crystals and recorded how the water responded to these exposures. The results are astounding.

His premise is that if our bodies are mostly made up of water and if outside influences alter water crystals then our very structure is affected by the bombardment of circumstances, choices, and catalysts, whether positive or negative.

We are nature and nature is us. The molecular structure of everything is basically the same. Whatever we do to the earth we do to ourselves.

This is not some treatise on environmentalism. This is simply being aware that our basic structure is made of the same elements as the earth itself. The elements of our bodies are affected by the same forces that affect the earth. Becoming attuned to the majesty of the world we live in gives us greater capacity to call upon these elements to assist our needs.

Be One with the Universe.

Lately science has even been able to break down the elements further to discover that when you go beyond the atoms' structure what you are left with is light. We are beings of light. Ancient scriptures allude to the light elements in a spiritual way. Perhaps the prophets knew more about our existence in a physical way than we give them credit for.

Whether they did or not, science has now proven that we are of the earth, so why not allow those elements to assist us in our life journey. What are the beauties of the sky, mountains, rivers, lakes, oceans, rolling hills, and vast plains, etc here for? Of course our very existence is dependent on what the earth can produce, from the food we eat to the clothes we wear, to the very air we breathe.

And what about the endorphins produced when we allow ourselves to experience the joy in the scenic benefits of the world around us? The clichéd phrase of "take time to smell the roses," is important to heed. If we will stop, even if it is only for a moment, and appreciate something beautiful we will be healthier, happier, and more emotionally stable.

Learn how to stop and allow the earth to rejuvenate you.

Chapter 13 - Take the Shoes from Off Your Feet

Do not deny the Divine Presence in your life. Allow God and angels to influence, inspire, assist, and safeguard. Spirituality is part of being. You need to incorporate all the instruments at your disposal to enable you to be successful in your life's journey.

Janie:

This chapter was remarkably challenging for me to put together. I had a feeling of reverence whenever I thought about it. I knew it was possibly the most important chapter I would write. I pondered, prayed and meditated over what should be in it from the beginning of the book. Every time I tried to put something down on paper I ended up being inspired about what to write in other chapters instead of this one. From the start of the project this particular chapter haunted me the most.

I was surprised at my inability to know what to say here. As a matter of fact I was shocked. The reason being, I am a spiritual person. I have no trouble traveling in a spiritual realm. I know God is a real person who loves me. When I started the book I had an idea what needed to be in every chapter except this one. I was sure it would come to me. It did not. The closer I got to the end of the book the more concerned I became over my inability to write about the Divine Presence in each one of our lives.

It is said, "That which is most valuable is the most difficult to obtain."

If that is true then conceivably this is the chapter of greatest essence. Perhaps this chapter if carefully digested will change your life in ways none of the other chapters can.

Janie:

I am not sure about the above statement. You must see for yourself.

The number 13 holds a defined impression in people's minds. Most of it is in a joking manner. For some people who are truly superstitious this number can be ominous. I wanted the information in this chapter to be significant. I wanted something to click. I want it to be ominous in a dynamic and life changing way. So I chose the number that perks up more heads than any other as the place to put this message. I did it so you would remember where this information is located in this book.

When at last I knew I had to write chapter thirteen I placed the opening paragraph where I would see it constantly and refused to allow myself to work on anything else until I came up with the core elixir to be distilled into it.

I say core elixir because Spirituality is an essence. You cannot see it, touch it, or taste it. You cannot hold it in your hand. You can see, touch, taste, and hold the results of it... but the 'It' is elusive. You cannot 'Google' it, do an internet search, download it on an 'ipad,' or buy it at the local mall or big box store.

After two weeks of searching and pondering it came to me. The reason I was having such a hard time is because... All Things are Spiritual to Me.

This chapter to me is sacred. Sometimes sacred things appear to be sappy or overly sentimental to outsiders. I don't mean outsiders as being people who don't belong here. I mean it in the terms of outside of my head... what I am seeing with my heart or my spiritual vision.

Bingo! ... That is what makes this chapter so formidable. It is because we all have spiritual eyes, but each person sees through these eyes in a little different manner. Each person's sacred vision is unique.

And a short caveat here is the inevitable problem that whenever a person seeks after the spiritual path, the Adversary throws stones. Negative influences of the world want to control us. They do not want us to experience the ultimate joy, which is spiritual in nature.

The negative influences insist that momentary fleeting blips of satisfaction distracting us from what is important or essential can counterfeit true joy. This keeps us in a continual state of discord.

Those negative voices tell us we are not capable, worthy, or worthwhile. We, the ordinary folk, are not talented. And, after all, what in the world can 'I' contribute to this life. I am just a nobody.

Your spiritual vision is in direct relationship to your own personal divine or spiritual experiences. Some people have had a lot of experience with this, while others have had only a little. And still there are some of you who have not realized it exists at all in your lives. For those of you who are unfamiliar with the Divine Presence or Spiritual Realm of your life, suspend your disbelief just for a few pages. Go back to your childhood when the wonder and awe of everything was a possibility.

"Oh," you say with a cynical sneer. That was before reality hit you, before you knew what the real world was all about. Time has hardened you. You were forced to 'grow up.' You have made mistakes, painful mistakes. You have been hurt by somebody. Someone has disappointed you. Your health has failed, maybe over and over. No matter how hard you try, your financial woes never get easier, and perhaps they are getting worse. Somebody you love is ill. And some of you have serious parent issues of various natures. Certainly a few of you have been abused, physically, or emotionally.

A few of you will experience all of the above scenarios and probably some we haven't mentioned before you are finished with your life's mission.

It all sounds pretty bleak.

Between the two of us, (Janie and Lyn) we have up to this point in our lives endured...

Death of a spouse; death of a child; bankruptcy; life threatening illness; life threatening illness of a child leaving that child with lifelong aftereffects; heart attack; pulmonary embolism; crippling accident; cancer; obesity; continued financial issues; wayward children with all their inherent problems; chronic health issues; divorce; unwarranted legal battles; and death of a grandchild.

Both of us laugh about the collection of trials we have racked up. And we are sure there are more where those came from. How can we make light of such things? And does making light of them diminish the trauma, heartache, sorrow, and ultimate reverence of what each experience gave to us?

The answer to the second question is, No. The answer to the first question could be the fact both of us have also had near death moments of our own in which each of their lives temporarily crossed over that line we call death.

Janie's first experience was a near drowning accident of being sucked into a log jam on the Snake River. Lyn's experience came when she was in critical condition from a serous health problem. The complications caused her to go into cardiac arrest and she stepped for a short time over from this life to the next. Janie claimed she must be a slow learner because she had a second experience during the birth of her number seven child. The epidural she received was placed too high and it affected the beating of her heart causing it to slow to a near stopping point.

Janie:

I know that all things denote there is a God. All things are sacred to me. The earth is sacred. Even rocks are sacred. People are sacred. The challenges of my life are sacred. I see God in every flower, tree, and blade of grass. I see Him in every animal, bird, and fish. I also see Him in every face of every person, every baby, child, teenager, young adult, middle aged, and those who reflect the wisdom of the ages.

I compare the probability of there not being a Divine Being to this... Print the Gettysburg Address. Paste each word on a piece of cardboard and put the pieces into a jar. Shake up the jar and dump out the words one at a time. The chance of randomly being able to shake out each word in its proper place in the text is about as likely as us showing up here in this life by chance.

And even if by some miracle a person could accomplish this feat I still know without a shadow of a doubt that there is an afterlife and that there is a God. I know because I have been there.

In the New Testament Jesus tells stories called Parables. These parables were tailored to raise consciousness and teach the people of their time period specific moral lessons. The ones who paid attention became enlightened. It is my belief that every experience of our own individual lives can teach some poignant lesson. If we step out and become an observer and look at the situations or stories we have day-to-day we can see in each event some personal private parable. The purpose of seeing our experiences as parables is to learn the lessons. This will raise each of us through those experiences to a higher point of enlightenment.

"Those who do not learn from the past are destined to relive it."

There are many versions of this saying. It appears in some form in numerous different cultures.

The admonition refers not only to past histories of peoples and cultures but also to your own life. Remember we told you earlier in this book, it isn't the questions you get right on the test that you remember it is the ones you get wrong. The greatest lessons are the ones we learn from our mistakes. God loves us so much He allows us to have these experiences to make our lives rich and full. It deepens our joy and appreciation for the good things, the good times, and the good people.

Time is a gift from God. He gives us a new minute every 60 seconds, and a new hour every 60 minutes. Every 24 hours we get a new day. Every seven days we get a new week, then we get new months, new years, and new decades. God wants us to feel like, no matter what, we can start over again and do better this time. Every day is a clean slate. It does not have to be marked up from yesterday unless we choose for it to be.

It is kind of like working out in the yard. Each spring you can plant a new garden. You till up last year's dirt, throw away the old weeds, and start fresh. Nobody wants to savor and transplant last year's weed seeds into this year's garden.

You get wet, sweaty, and muddy. You also tear your shirt, split your pants, and ruin your shoes. Maybe the sole of one shoe even separates and flaps back and forth when you walk. When you come into the house, you remove your clothes, and take a shower. God has laid out brand new clothes on the bed for you to wear.

Would you say, "No thanks, I will just put the ruined, wet, sweaty, muddy stuff back on." After you put your dirty clothes back on would you look up and say, "Now let's go to the theater," "out to dinner," or "to church?" This is a ludicrous idea. We would not think of doing that.

The greatest joys and/or relief come after we have struggled through some crisis, problem, or situation. We did it. We survived. We will be okay. When it is over God gives us the new clothes of experience.

God is always in the details. Sometimes it is hard to find Him, but He is there.

Janie:

I'm not Jewish but it is my understanding that there is an ancient Jewish tradition that there is a blessing in everything. And it is our responsibility to recognize whatever that blessing is. (Even if it is not an old Jewish tradition I think it is a good idea.)

Women giving birth is a grand example of this concept. After an arduous labor that last and final push propels the baby from the safety of womb into mortality. Quite often the release of that pressure and pain coupled with the miracle of new life sends the mother into a euphoric high that cannot be matched through any other experience.

Lyn:

I find it impossible to deny God's existence when I think of the miracle of birth, the mysteries of the oceans, or the depth of the human mind. I have heard the arguments of scholars and scientists--they shout from their papers and books, "Here is proof,... how can you believe God exists?"

I watch daily an osprey tending her young or a grandchild singing a song and I shout back to the naysayers, "How can you not?"

Our survey held a myriad of answers to our question, 'where do you go to find peace?' We made a list for you of some of their answers. Perhaps you will agree with a few of them or maybe you will consider trying a new place, or you might simply realize a place of peace for you that you had not previously recognized.

God loves you and He will give you peace when you seek it. He will give you peace in the midst of chaos, pain, suffering, and trials, if you ask Him for it.

"Where do I go to find peace"...

To my grandmother... church... bed... my coffee shop

To a cup of tea... a river... my rock... I ride my bike

I play soothing music... go to the zoo... my mother... my tree

To my inner silence... I scrapbook... out in a field

Anywhere alone

I watch a favorite movie

I read… spend time in my kitchen…a park… my bedroom

Bubble bath… my cabin… the mountains… swim

I sing… I breathe deeply… I go to my favorite chair… my garden

A lake… my front porch… my best friend's home… shopping

To my husband… go for a walk… Central Park… camping

To my sister, father, brother, son, daughter, mother… my journal

A drive in the country… to the World Trade Center Memorial…my garden

My computer… I go running… on a picnic… to a bird sanctuary

I sit down and play with my children… to a bookstore… look at a photo album

I telephone an old friend… work in my yard… watch or play a sport

My plush robe, a cup of cocoa and my fireplace… my old farm house

Anywhere my grandchildren are… to a wise older friend… a councilor

To the cemetery… to my memories… anywhere there are people…

To the grocery store where everyone knows my name

Lyn:

In the mid-sixties I had a poster hanging in my bedroom of a beautiful sunset on the ocean. Printed over the water were these words;

I believe in the sun even when it's not shining:

I believe in love even when I am alone:

I believe in God even when He is silent…

We have all had prayers that were not answered in the way we hoped. Sometimes we feel that a plea has not been answered at all. What happens to faith when we are greeted with silence?

Perhaps you are stronger than I am, but sometimes I feel cheated. Self-pity triggers my whining and I am miserable. In this mood I make everyone around me feel depressed too. When this anxiousness comes over me I go to a place that brings me peace. There, I find my center again and I take one more step forward. God loves us. He is always here for us. He is always right next to you. He never pulls away. It is you and I who pull away from Him! It is as easy as speaking out loud or thinking a thought that will bring Him into our consciousness once again.

We are all so precious to Him. He wants us to succeed in our endeavors. He wants us to have Joy in Our Journey! As we talk with Him we bring His presence to our lives. We are then present in His blessings to us. It is through this state we are able to enjoy the presents or gifts He brings or bestows upon us each and every day. We are invited to this party and we only have to open the package to receive the gifts God wants to share with us today. Tomorrow we ask again, and He always shares His blessings. Being present with God is a choice we must make daily.

God wants us to succeed more than Satan wants us to fail.

Many ladies in our survey expressed inadequacy about their spirituality. They felt it necessary to spell out a list of flaws in their character. They were more comfortable with talking about their faults and their weaknesses instead of claiming their strengths.

Perhaps this is a kind of humility. However the idea of it is actually a bit disturbing. Throughout the history of this world we as woman have taken second chair so to speak, to men. Is this the reason so many are hesitant to speak? We are the ones who will teach our children and grandchildren. This hesitation or restriction is self-imposed. God does not want us to be silent. He has a specific place for both men and women, neither is greater or more important than the other.

How can He help if we don't knock? Too many of us feel that we cannot say we are spiritual beings. A few of us think spirituality is a cop-out. Others think it is just plain silly, a bit awkward, and embarrassing.

Some of us think we cannot claim spirituality until we have done every single thing we think or perceive God sent us on earth to do. But guess what? It ain't gonna happen! Life is a process, not a goal. Process takes time. Are you not wiser than you were ten years ago, or yesterday?

God knows your heart.

He knows you are not perfect. That is one of the reasons we came to this earth so we could learn of the imperfections in our character. He loves you in spite of your imperfections and because of them.

Let Him lead you along. Plead with Him to help you. Do not assume you know His path for you. Ask, and then the most important thing…. Listen.

His voice comes to you in many ways, a thought, a dream, an impression, or an inspiration through the actions or words of another. You will know it is His voice because there will come a warming peace, a comforting spirit that will withstand the doubts and naysayers of your own misgivings and those of others. It will be a familiar feeling. You will know you have felt it before and you will want to feel it again and again.

Lyn:

The night my first husband died I was taken immediately to the hospital where he had been life-flighted. He had been gone for over an hour before he got to the hospital. He died saving the lives of three co-workers in an accident at work. C02 had dumped into a building. My husband being large in stature and in heart carried or assisted each of these men out. Somebody thought there was still someone inside so he went back in again. My husband was the only one that died.

When I reached his side he simply looked asleep. I had three terrifying hours alone with him until my children and other close family could get there. The first hour I begged him to breathe. I laid my head on his chest and pleaded with him and God to let him take a breath.

The second hour I spent alone with him, I screamed, ranted, and raved. I told him and God that I simply could not survive this. I could not possibly go on and help our children survive without the father they worshiped. I told him it should have been me; the four kids all loved their dad so much and relied on him. I begged God to take me instead, because the kids needed him more. I sobbed and said that I could not go on without him.

The third hour I sat still and stared at him, knowing that my prayers were not going to be answered in the ways I wanted them to be. I slowed my breathing, my breath, the only breath in that cold room. Now, in a much softer, humble voice, I asked the right question. "How? I said to my husband, "How do I go on without you?" It was then I heard his deep rich voice say softly in my ear, "One step at a time, Babe, just one step at a time..."

I am not going to tell you that it got easier after that. It was and still is the hardest thing I have ever gone through, but that is how process works. We are never finished grieving or loving or learning and that is the way it is meant to be. That is how life and death work, One Step at a Time.

We did not come here to prove who God is. We came here to "proof" who we are. God knows who He is and He knows who we are. He wants us to find out who we are. This happens through our trials and life experiences. He wants us to try harder, to do better, to subject our wills to His refiners fire and 'proof' our souls. He loves us more than we can possibly imagine. His mercy is infinitely greater than our ability to comprehend. He loves us more than we love ourselves.

And what about the difference between 'here' and 'there?'

If you read the accounts of near death experiences very carefully, or if you have had one of these yourself and you can remember the details, where does the person go?

Yes, she goes into another realm but where is that realm? It is not very far away. It actually is right here with us. Maybe for some of those who die, perhaps they have the opportunity to leave this earthly realm and travel to other places. But the accounts relayed by those who have gone there and have come back, report an existence right here among, around, and intermingled with all of us mortals.

There have also been numerous accounts of angels seen or felt helping, inspiring, comforting, and warning mortals. Often these angels are known to the person receiving the visitation. Many times the angel is a family member or close friend. This supports the evidence that for the most part we do stick around here and help others once we 'cross over.'

Janie:

My daughter, Sarah, was totally a mama's baby. She would not go to anybody else but me. She was probably the only one of my children who preferred me to her dad. She was shy and reserved, that is until we moved into 'the old house.' A grandmotherly neighbor came over and suddenly Sarah who had just turned two years old was all over this woman. If the woman came into our house Sarah would climb into her lap and do embarrassing things like turn her head and look into her ears, squeeze her cheeks and squint into the lady's eyes. She even would look down her blouse in the front and in the back. This behavior was so out of character for Sarah that I was shocked.

The lady was gracious and told me she loved the attention and she loved Sarah. I shouldn't worry about it. But the bizarre behavior did not go away. I wondered if I was not giving my daughter enough physical attention, so one day after the lady left I gathered Sarah into my arms and sat down with her on the couch.

"Oh Sarah," I said, "I love you so much."

Sarah was my earliest and best young talker. She looked up into my eyes and said, "I love you too, Mama. Was that our other Grandma?"

My heart froze. I knew what was going on, but could not believe it so I had to validate my suspicions. However, in that moment there was some kind of spirit to spirit communication and I was enlightened. I absolutely knew. Still I had to ask. (We mortals are always looking for tangible proof of spiritual things).

"What other Grandma?" I said blinking through the tears now swimming across my vision.

"You know, Mama, the Grandma who used to visit us when we lived in all those other houses," Sarah rubbed her hand on my face and peered intently into my eyes. "It's okay, Mama, don't cry."

Because my husband was a home builder in the first years of our marriage we built and sold and built and sold. All of the homes were in the same general area. Grandma Belle was a second mother to me. She took care of me and taught me and loved me. However she was diagnosed with cancer shortly after we were married. She would come to the city and have various cancer treatments and then stay with me for a day or two. She was the grandmother who stayed with us in all those other houses.

The problem was Sarah was not born yet. She was not born until after my grandmother died. Most of my other children were also not born yet, and the ones who were born were too young to know of, or remember her visits. Being only two years old Sarah was too young to have heard any conversations about this grandmother's visitations. Besides I don't recall we ever discussed the fact of Grandma Belle coming to stay with us. It just never came up in conversation.

You can think whatever you want but I have had too many personal experiences not to know that the spirit world is right here with us. I know most assuredly that there was a life before this and that there is a life after this one. And I know that God will greet us there in person as will those we love who have gone on before us. And perhaps some of our posterity yet to come will be there as well.

God has given us this great life to discover and refine our individual Power and our individual Light.

You are Power. And you are Light.

If women understood and then engaged their full Power, the illumination would free humanity from all the ills, all the sorrows, all the pain, all the suffering, and all the heartaches found in this life.

Your Power and your Light can heal the world.

How plausible is this concept?

That which we truly believe will surely come to pass, if not today then tomorrow, if not tomorrow then in the eternities to come.

If one million women believed the concepts we have discussed and through their positive energy and example they each convinced one more woman to believe and this continued one person convincing one more each year. It would take less than 16 years and the entire population of women in the world would believe. The positive energy generated from that kind of believing would bring about complete world peace.

So you say, "I am not a million women. I am only one."

Okay, if only one women believed these concepts and shared them with only one other person each year and this continued on for twenty years. It would mean this message would have been shared with 1,046,528 women. What is the value of one life, of one person having a knowledge that God is real, and that He loves her? An understanding that there is a life after this one, that her prayers will be answered, that she can have peace in the midst of chaos, and that she has a Divine purpose and mission in this life, is the fulfillment of this purpose.

God saves us one at a time. He knows your name. If He called you across a digital platform like a cell phone, ipad, or some other electronic device, you would recognize His voice. Attune your spiritual ears to hear His voice when he calls you through spiritual phone lines.

Janie:

While I was in Morocco, Lyn and I were having lunch with a Western Saharan Muslim grandmother named Rabia. We laughed and told stories and had great food. Suddenly Rabia made the hand sign that represented Alla or God to her. She raised her hand straight up with the fingers pointing heavenward.

"We have the same God," she said, "My God of Abraham is the same God as your God of Abraham." (Lyn and I were both raised as Christians and she knew that).

And then she touched her hand on her heart and in turn touched both mine and Lyn's hearts.

She was right. We may call Him by different names but we all worship the same God. We must unite our faith, belief, and trust in that God.

Women of the world you are Powerful beyond your wildest dreams. You are Powerful beyond belief. God knows you and loves you and wants you to be happy. He wants you to have Joy. With God on your side and the help of your angels everything is possible.

"Take the shoes from off your feet for the place where you stand is Holy ground."

Chapter 14 - I Love These Shoes!

Choose Joy... Always choose Joy.

It is a choice. You may not choose the circumstances you must endure in this life but you can choose the attitude, the way you perceive them, and how you will deal with those circumstances. No matter what... Always choose Joy.

Yeah Right... That is easy for you to say.

I can't pay my bills.

I suffer from depression.

I lost my job.

I can't have a baby.

I am stuck home with a bunch of little kids.

My car broke down.

My husband lost his job.

My mother has Alzheimer's.

My husband left me.

Somebody cheated me.

My son/daughter is breaking my heart.

I was just diagnosed with cancer, or some other dreaded disease.

I have an ingrown toenail.

You are right. It is difficult if nearly impossible to choose joy. Every day there is something to cry about. We agree it is hard work.

But Choose Joy anyway!

Janie:

I did not know how exquisite the physical pain of my daughter's sudden death could possibly be. Sarah was drop dead gorgeous. As a baby people stopped me in stores to go get their husband/wife/mother etc. to come see this beautiful baby. Her beauty never waned not in looks nor in spirit. Then she was gone, in an instant just gone. Accidents happen for her it was an automobile accident involving five teenagers who pulled out from a breakfast café to get back to school on time and in their haste they pulled in front of a semi-tractor-trailer accelerating to merge onto the freeway. My chest ached. Some days the actual tormenting pain was so great I was exhausted. My heart hurt. The center of my body felt like I had been shot. There it was a ragged gaping hole and nothing to fill it. No bandage to cover it, no sutures to close it, and no medicine to dull it.

The morning after she died I was overwhelmed when I woke up to feel such pain. I had close family members who died before Sarah did, but none of them evoked the heartache of losing my child. Still, I thought I could handle it. Okay, I said to myself. I have to allow this grieving process to take place and I guess this pain is just part of the package.

The funeral was over. We resumed our life but the pain was still there. Day after day my heart still hurt. At first the pain dulled the shock of Sarah being gone. Suddenly, without warning, the sunshine in our lives was obliterated by the dark suffocating cloud of death. The physical pain in my body kept me from the pain of knowing she would not ever be there again for Christmas, Easter, or family vacations. However, life does go on and I needed to figure out a way to go on as well.

Each morning I would wake up and then I would remember and then there it was again... the pain. It walked around with me day after day. Wherever I went it went there with me.

At first I accepted it. Then I became angry about it. I blamed it on Sarah's death. I was angry she climbed into that car and went to breakfast with her friends. She shouldn't have gone. If she had not died I would not hurt so much.

Then I reasoned if I never had Sarah, if she had never been born, I would not have this pain. For a short time I wished I did not know who Sarah was. This made me feel like a horrible mother and the pain intensified.

The next thing I blamed the pain on was the futility of life. Sarah's death was one more devastation in a long line of tragic bad luck hitting my life and my family one unfortunate event right after another.

From March of 1997 to March of 1998 a lot of things happened. I had Sarah's funeral and then three of my children were married. (Hmmmn... A funeral and three weddings, I think somebody made a movie with a title sounding something like that.) There was not a lot of time to enjoy a good long 'Pity Party.' I had too much to do. I tried to ignore the pain and stay focused on what was ahead. I was sure this technique would make it go away. It did not.

It was while I was sorting pictures for my daughter's wedding video that the "Aha Moment" struck.

The day Sarah died her brothers and sisters took all of her school pictures and lined them up in chronological order across the front of the piano. Before Sarah died each day when she came home from school, she played the piano. We always knew what kind of day she had by what and how she played. The kids thought it a fitting gesture to leave the photos there even after the funeral was over. Every morning after that when I walked past the piano I shed a tear or two when I saw her pictures. It was, however, comforting for the children, so I left them.

Now I was sitting on the floor near the piano with boxes of the past dumped out all around me trying to organize Rachel's life story for her wedding video. Rachel was at that time attending college in Hawaii.

She would not be home until a month before her wedding took place. I missed her terribly.

Sorting the various pictures into piles according to age I followed the memories like Alice in Wonderland down the rabbit hole of my past into the world of bottles, babies, and barefoot children playing in the sun. The piano full of heartache and the floor full of paper disappeared into backyard tent villages made from bedsheets, kid-produced movies, birthday parties, and camping trips. I entered the photos. I felt the rain, the mud, and the mayhem.

Suddenly I realized I was clutching a bunch of pictures to my heart and crying so hard I lost the focus. It all disappeared. The magic was gone. The babies were gone. The tent sheets were all washed and folded in the cupboards. Rachel was grown and I was alone. Right in front of me on the floor I saw Rachel's school photos laid out in the same order as Sarah's photos on the piano right above me. Why was I crying over Rachel's pictures? She wasn't dead.

And then the great epiphany... All of the Sarahs smiling down at me from the piano were gone before Sarah died just like all the Rachels in the pictures I was holding were also gone to the places where dreams come from. The little girl, Rachel, was just as gone as the little girl, Sarah. Now granted the big girl, Rachel, was very much alive and perhaps would still be here to create more memories where the big girl, Sarah, had entered a realm where I will have to wait to see what she has been doing. But the memories of both girls are just the same. They are stored in the photos, and the stories, and the hearts of all of us and we can visit them any time we wish through the travel medium of the mind.

I picked up a snapshot of Sarah shortly before her death. It was Christmas she was laughing. Her hand was raised, her magnificent hands. How I had envied those hands. She had long slender fingers that caressed piano keys and babies in the same way. I was so afraid I would forget her hands. And then I knew... I was holding onto the pain *because I was afraid I would forget. Every morning when I woke up I would remember and then I would feel the pain. I was choosing pain.*

In the beginning the pain served a purpose. It helped me get through the death and the process of death. Once I got through all of that I was choosing pain because I was afraid I would forget. I was afraid to let it go. In a sort of convoluted way if I let it go I felt I would be letting Sarah go. None of this was a conscious thing. I did not do it intentionally. It just happened.

None of us think we are choosing to be miserable. In a sort of mixed up way we think we have to suffer in order to be accepted. Have you ever noticed what people say when something really good happens? For example when somebody gets a new car all you hear are the excuses of why that person had no other choice. She HAD to, or was FORCED to buy the car in question.

Sally: It looks like you got a new car?

Jill: I didn't have any choice. I had to buy it. I was driving down the road in my old car and first the bumper fell off and then the engine dropped out. My next door neighbor told me that if I wanted a new car there was a dealer who would only sell a car to a woman on Tuesday. So I rushed right over there and the man tied me up and threatened to sell my first born if I didn't buy the third car on the right. So I had no choice. And that's how come I've got this new car.

Sally: Oh man, you were so lucky. It's a good thing it all happened on Tuesday or who knows where you'd be.

It is bizarre that we can't just rejoice with each other. Why is it so difficult to say, "Wahoo! I just got a new car!" and everybody cheers… no condemnation. Nobody says behind the person's back, "Wasn't she on welfare last month?"

It doesn't matter.

Life is hard. Let's not make it harder. Find comfort in the chaos. There are always surprises in the sunshine. We can find rest in the rain. And joy is in the journey.

It does not betray the burden to laugh while you carry it. When you are climbing a mountain nobody ever said you could not stop and enjoy the view on the way to the top. Happy people are healthier. Smiles are contagious. When you see somebody smile you get an instant blip of joy. It does not even matter if the person is smiling at you, or at someone else, or something else, the joy transfers immediately. God wants you to be happy. Choose Joy!

Do not get bogged down with the media that is filled with doom and gloom. Find things to laugh about. Find things to make you happy. No matter how depressing, painful, or serious your situations are find something to make you smile.

Joy is not in things, it is in us.

Lyn:

Joy is one of my favorite words. I keep Christmas decorations up year-round with the word Joy on them.

Are joy and happiness easy to attain or maintain?

Maintaining joy--all the time--never ending--is not realistic. It is not possible to maintain joy every hour of every day. That would be like eating a decadent flourless chocolate cake for every meal. Not only would we get tired of it... eventually that much dessert would make us very ill. Rather we savor moments of joy. It is the reward. It is our survival. It is where we go when we want to luxuriate in the memories.

Take a piece of paper and jot down a brief recall of joyful experiences in your past. It will make you happy just thinking about them.

Now let's talk about attaining joy. Can you attain joy? You bet! First of all you must decide what invokes joy inside of you.

Here's a list a few of our favorites to help get you started.

A glorious sunset or sunrise

Holding a newborn

Snuggling next to my husband

Holding hands at the movies

Listening to a child read

Hearing a baby giggle

A flower garden

A shade tree, a hammock, and a good book

When you are having a particularly problematic day, stop yourself, look at the sky, think of a past joyful moment, or read something uplifting even if it is just a short quote. In other words do not let a day go by without finding joy somewhere or from something.

Keep a humble perspective. Your sorrow could possibly have been another woman's joy.

Janie:

My sister gave birth to a handicapped son. He was flown to a children's hospital where the news just got more discouraging by the minute. I sat with her for long hours in the waiting room of the Intensive Care Unit. Because of the serious nature of his care each hour she had only a few moments to be with her baby.

One heart-breaking day of hearing about the permanency of some of Casey's conditions, my sister was crying when the time came for her to spend her few minutes inside the care unit. As she walked through the doors another young mother walked out with her husband. I saw the husband tell her to wait for him right there and he left. This lady leaned her head against the wall as she watched my sister crying as she passed through the large unit doors. The lady looked at me. I offered the lady an explanation, "Her son is paralyzed," I said.

She paused and then replied, "My son is dead."

It doesn't matter what your circumstances are there will always be somebody in a worse situation and there will always be somebody who is better off. Do not compare your worst to somebody else's best. And do not ever compare your best to someone else's worst. The bottom line here is plain and simply... do not compare!

In this game of life some days you are ahead and others you are behind and so is everybody else.

Lyn:

I had been running so fast and furiously that I had almost forgotten how to relax. And then the question suddenly came to me. "How will I ever be able to write honestly and sincerely about enjoying the journey if I can't do it myself?"

I believe wholeheartedly in the importance of enjoying our journey. I have moments of it, but I wonder how our lives would be different if we consistently on a daily basis took the time to enjoy moments, big moments, little moments, seemingly insignificant moments? How would our lives change for the better?

For years one of my favorite fantasies was to have a whole day to myself to write, read, and explore the passions and interests of my heart.

In my recent travels I have had that time and instead of doing what I thought I would do I found myself spending those precious moments missing my family, my river, my home, my things, and my friends. In other words I am never satisfied. And the worst part of the whole thing is that I want to be satisfied. I want to look back on this time of my life and realize how fortunate I have been. I want to remember these quiet times and realize how perfect they were. I want to remember every nuance of each of my grandbabies' faces and the tender way in which my husband gazes at me while I read. I must remember seeing my country garden in bloom, my cat lying in the sun, and a million other things.

I am tired of expecting too much and demanding too much of others and myself. I want to relax and enjoy this day as a perfect gift from God. This is the time to enjoy whatever gifts God chooses to give me today. I truly want to have joy in my life today, and tomorrow, but most importantly I have to enjoy it today.

We all have certain routines about how we process through each day. We have discussed this in Chapter 10. What happens when the day is not going according to the routine or the plan?

First thing... Don't stress.

Take a minute to stop and see why it is not going according to the plan? Is this an everyday interruption or is it just today? Does the plan need to be adjusted?

It takes twenty-one days to alter, change, start up, or get rid of a habit. If the plan needs to change for some reason, give yourself time.

However, some days are just plain "Fruit Basket Tipped Over" days.

When you were a kid did you ever play the game, Fruit Basket Tipped Over? It goes like this: Everybody sits in circle and is assigned to be a fruit. You must have at least two of each fruit sitting in your circle. Instead of counting out with numbers you do it with fruit names. Player number one is apple, number two is orange, number three is pear, number four is banana, number five is apple, and it all repeats until every person is assigned a fruit.

One player stands in the center and calls out the name of a fruit ie: Apple! All the apple players must jump up and take the seat of another apple player before the center person takes the open seat.

If the center player yells, "Fruit basket tipped over!" all the players must change seats. And they cannot change with somebody sitting next to them. This creates a chaotic pandemonium usually resulting in hysterical laughter and playful interactions.

Nobody ever wins. Eventually you set a time limit and just stop playing the game.

This is the way lots of days happen. The day starts with everything assigned a specific name or order, however as the day progresses the day becomes more and more chaotic. So let it. Step out of the picture for an insightful glance and just let the fruit basket tip over. Some of these can be your very best days. If nothing else they give you the fodder for future stories to laugh about. Choose Joy in the moment.

Loose the "School" mentality. Nobody is going to give you a grade at the end of the day. You don't have to start at the beginning of the book and take the chapters in consecutive order. You are not going to fail.

Janie:

This was a hard concept for me to accept. I was a good student in school and I delighted in the challenge of getting all the work done the right way, or going the extra mile to get the better grade. As I grew up I anticipated all the firsts I had to look forward to: My first date; first kiss; engagement; wedding day; reception; first night; first home; first meal; first child.

Somehow I had no concept of second. I was always striving to be first. Second had no place in my thought process.

When all my firsts were over I had no place to go. There wasn't any teacher there praising my performance with "Good job.. see kids... I want all of you to do it like Janie did."

I could not go to the office and pick up my report card and see how many "A's" I had.

I set personal goals of achievement and performance. At first I kept up with the routines and challenges I had placed before myself. The problem came when my house began to fill up with non-compliant people. Babies needed feeding, changing, and clean-up at all hours of the day and night. Children came home with some huge project they had forgotten about and now had to have it finished by morning on the most inconvenient of days.

And then there was a husband. I was amazed at how completely indifferent he was to things I felt were absolutes about my own personally perceived rules of accomplishment. I had grown up with a Dad and brother but somehow that did not give me any insight into how the male mind differed from mine.

One day my air conditioner was broken. It was the middle of July and hot as Hades. I was eight plus months pregnant. My neighbor, who was not pregnant and I were sitting under a skimpy little tree watching our kids play in the water. We had been there most of the day. I had been rehearsing a diatribe of things I hadn't done that day.

"Tell me," I said to my friend, "are you more or less productive when you are pregnant?"

She burst out laughing, "How can a person be less productive than doing nothing which is what we have done all day?"

"Janie," she continued, "You are not in school anymore. Nobody is going to send you to the principal's office if you spend one day sitting in the grass playing with your kids."

There it was. She had given me permission to not follow my routine. Up to that point in my life I had no idea I needed someone to give me permission. Her comment hit me with a jolt. It came back over and over again. Let go of the school mentality.

But I am a slow learner and years later I was again pregnant. It was again summer. I was living in a different house in a different town, but the problem was the same. My air conditioning was out of order. I spent the day passing out popsicles and towels to the kids who were in some form of water playing all day.

A friend stopped by to pick up her child. As we stood watching the children squealing under the hose waterfall they had rigged up I *replayed all the things I had not done that day. I concluded with, "I haven't done one productive thing this whole day."*

My friend said, "Of course you have. You have done the most productive thing you have to do at this very moment in time. You have spent the entire day making a baby."

She whistled to her child, wrapped her in a towel, set her in the car and they left.

Again I was reminded, "You are not in school anymore. It is okay to deviate from the norm."

She had given me an incredible gift. I had taken this marvelous experience of co-creation with God for granted. She grounded me. She gave me permission to take Joy in my Journey.

We give you permission…

To wear your most comfy pair of shoes no matter what they look like

To let go of your school mentality

To deviate from your regular routine

To play with a child

To laugh

To cry

To be humble

To be grateful

To travel back into your memory and spend some quality time there

To let it all go

To just have a good ole' Fruit Basket Tipped Over day

And to find Joy in the Journey of all of it

Chapter 15 - I Want Shoes That Fly!

Expect Miracles. Be open to the fact that every day miracles are happening all around you. See the miracles in your life and expect them to multiply. Work for them, and then give credit to that higher power that allowed them to happen.

Janie:

Our finances were depleted. Robert had made an appointment. We were supposed to be signing some papers. He has always lived a real life Monopoly game of buying properties and building houses. I thought he was changing his clothes I found him lying on the bed. Instead of going to the bank I drove him to the hospital. By the time we arrived he was in full cardiac arrest. After dynamic efforts his heart started to beat again. He was in combative coma. His heart had been stopped too long... oxygen depletion... brain trauma. Things looked bleak at best. All night he was on a machine that did his breathing for him. He was transferred to a major heart hospital.

Three days blurred by as one long slogging murky mess of quicksand, listening to and watching machines ticking, beeping, and breathing for my husband. The next examination, another test, new depressing diagnoses, all behind masks of smiling faced health care professionals trained to deliver bad news like politicians at a news briefing.

At home ten children still had to eat, go to school, and be reassured. My youngest broke out with chicken pox. The quagmire sucked me deeper as I struggled to breathe. My circumstances had taken form, a looming monster like the bad genie in the movie of Aladdin towered over me "I have all the power. And I am going to destroy you, ha ha ha."

I was broke. It was more than money. It was despair. I did the best I could. I tried to be a good girl, a good wife, a good mother, yet for some cosmic reason I felt like the poster child for problems. For years we had gone from one crazy devastating situation to another. And now, if my husband died, no life insurance, no income, no assets, only a little old turn of the century house with a mortgage and ten kids to raise. If he lived it appeared he would have massive brain damage. I could not allow myself to think about any of this right now. I had to get my children off to school and myself to the hospital.

As I left the house I noticed the desk where my husband was working just before all of this mess started, there was the pile of bills he was sorting through. I vaguely remember him telling me we needed $1,200 right now to pay them, but we had no money.

When I arrived at the hospital he was sleeping. Down the hall from his room I took the opportunity to slip into the hospital chapel. Nobody was there. I dropped to my knees and prayed telling God in great detail all about my woes. I ended the prayer with, "I think I need $1,200 right now and I have nothing and no way to get anything. Could you please either tell me what to do or else send me the money so I can stay here with Robert."

Think back to a time when you truly believed in fairy tales, Santa Claus, or the idea you could really live happily ever after. Do you still believe? If not, why?

Everybody loves to hear a story about an impossible dream coming true, a down-and-outer making good, or a person's triumph against all odds. We love to cheer for the underdog. Why?

It is because deep down inside we are all the underdog. We are creatures of hope. We envision ourselves as each one of those people. We want to believe if it could happen to the other guy, maybe it will happen for me. Daniel Gilbert, Professor of Psychology, and author of the book, **Stumbling on Happiness,** suggests that by nature human beings tend to think of future events in an overly optimistic way.

In other words whether we realize it or not, we expect miracles. The odd thing about this is we expect they will happen to the other guy. When they happen to us we are surprised.

Janie:

Over the weekend at the hospital friends and neighbors began visiting as word passed through our small community about Robert's condition. They all brought get-well cards. Since Robert was in intensive care there was no place to set them so I slipped each one into my bag and saved them to read later when I was alone.

I told my son who worked for us to bring all the bills on Robert's desk to the hospital so we could see exactly how much money I needed and decide what I could do about them. He arrived while I was opening the cards. Each friend and neighbor had put a bit of money in his or her card. The amount of money came to exactly $1,200. We paid every bill and I had $30 leftover. I used this money to buy myself food while I stayed at the hospital with my husband. My neighbors took care of my children. One neighbor, a live alone nurse, took a couple of days off to care for my chicken poxed son.

That which we truly believe will surely come to pass, if not today then tomorrow, if not tomorrow then in the eternities to come.

The truth is miracles are happening all around us every day. All we have to do is open our eyes to see and appreciate them.

People have a tendency to discount events. They fail to see the miracle as it unfolds. The person explains it away as the natural or expected outcome, or the coincidence, or perhaps a happy accident, or an unusual, or amazing situation. Miracles were a product of biblical times. It is silly to think they are still happening today. Or is it?

What is a miracle? Maybe the problem is people are simply uneducated in the knowledge of what a miracle is.

Webster's Dictionary says a miracle is: 'An event or action that apparently contradicts known scientific laws and is hence thought to be due to supernatural causes; an act of God, a remarkable event or thing, a marvel, or a wonderful example.'

This discussion is not complete without also examining the definition of synchronicity.

In the 1950's Carl Jung discovered an amazing phenomena while working with a patient in psychotherapy. Apparently the woman had a dream involving a golden scarab. While she is recounting this event to the good doctor an insect hit against Jung's cabinet window. Jung caught it and discovered to his surprise that it was indeed a golden scarab. This type of insect was very rare to that particular location.

As a result of this bizarre coincidence Jung was able to use the situation to help this woman overcome her problems. He called it synchronicity. He deemed it a form of a miracle. It was a beginning of his awareness of seemingly unrelated coincidences in people's lives that resulted in significant outcomes. The more aware he became of the process the more the process manifested itself… One could say the more those occurrences became apparent.

In other words as a person submits to the possibility of miracles, the more miracles show up in that person's life.

Most of the time the problem comes when you focus your attention on one particular miracle you 'want' to happen. You want it to happen exactly how, when, and where you imagine it. Miracles seldom happen this way. As a result you become discouraged and think you have been left out. Nobody sprinkled you with miracle pixie dust. For some reason the Fairy Godmother visited the ugly stepsisters this time and missed you and Cinderella.

Janie:

After a very scary two weeks, many prayers in his behalf, and a heart surgery, my husband experienced a miraculous recovery. We were humbled and grateful for this miracle however the fact remained we were still financially broke. Going out of the home to work was not an option for me at this time for a lot of reasons. I came up with the idea of growing a garden to help feed our family.

Carefully I scoured the house for all the possible coins and stashed cash I could treasure hunt from the couches, chairs, and cookies jars. I purchased seeds, some seedlings, and one container of plant food. I took an old three ringed binder wrote in today's date and recorded what I had purchased.

Every morning I got up before the children and spent time in the garden. I talked to the seeds and plants. I told them how much I needed their cooperation and help to feed my children. This is where the admonitions in chapters 9 and 12 helped me. Our finances did not really improve during this time. Our problems did not really diminish. I wanted the miracle of prosperity to open the front door and come in and help us out. In some ways the problems became more complex because of the recent medical issues. We added cardiac rehab to our daily routine. The plants, however, responded to my pleadings. They grew with enthusiasm. In fact an older gentleman neighbor who was a master gardener came over one day and saw the size of my tomato plants. He was shocked and amazed.

"What are you doing with this garden?" he asked. "My plants are half this size."

When I told him the only thing I was doing was talking to my plants he asked me to come and talk to his garden or at the very least share with him the secret words I was using.

Then one morning I was pulling the garden hose down the aisle between the rows and it coiled up in the middle. I yanked it hard. The hose flipped up like a disturbed snake and landed on top of my beautiful zucchini plant splitting it right through the middle. I know most people hate zucchini but my children love it. They will eat it any of a dozen different ways. I was counting on those zucchinis. I desperately needed those zucchinis. It happened so quickly I was momentarily stunned. I dropped down into the dirt next to my beloved plant, caressed a leaf with my hand, stroked it, and cried. "I am so sorry. I am so sorry. I am so sorry." It was all I could say over and over. I noticed large droplets of zucchini tears weeping out of the gaping crack severing the plant in two. I knew it would die.

I grabbed the plant and pushed it back together. Maybe I could make a plant tourniquet. Holding the plant together with one arm I pulled large dirt clods up around the base until there were enough of them to hold the zucchini precariously together. I ran to the outer edges of the garden and carried more solid clods to make my base stronger.

When I finished doing all I could do I knelt next to the plant. Taking the leaves in my hands I prayed. I told God how much I loved this zucchini plant, how much care I had taken to tend it. I asked God to see how much the plant loved me by growing so abundantly. I told my Heavenly Father how much I needed the zucchinis it would produce to feed my family. I even told Him about how many ways my children would eat the zucchinis. I prayed for God to save its life and allow it to produce for me, for my children, for itself.

Within a week the zucchini plant had been healed. It literally grew back together. I have never seen a plant heal like this one or produce like this zucchini plant did. I did not waste one single zucchini. If I had more than I could use, I made zucchini bread or some other dish and shared it with a neighbor. As a matter of fact I fed my family almost entirely from the garden that season. I kept a log of what I would have spent purchasing the harvest. Every time I picked something I matched it to what it currently cost at the local grocery store. The savings amounted to hundreds of dollars.

The miracle of the zucchini plant changed my life.

For some reason Robert and I and our family needed to go through the struggles we were experiencing at that time. There was something for us to learn, to do, or to accomplish. I am not sure what it was. We did not get the miracle of our troubles melting away like I had hoped. But the miracle of the zucchini plant was absolute proof somebody was watching over me. Somebody was making sure my little family was going to survive. I believe God used a simple zucchini plant to tell me He knew who I was and that he cared about what my heartaches were. It was truly as mighty a miracle for me in my day as it was in biblical times for Moses to roll back the Red Sea. And as I reread that Bible story about Moses I noticed that his troubles did not end with that miracle either.

There are big miracles, life saving, life altering obvious miracles. And then there are the quiet seemingly unimportant miracles. Sometimes it is the quiet ones that really sustain us. Most of the time we are unaware of their presence. We take the day-to-day events of our lives for granted. We have no idea how many times there has been Divine intervention and our lives have been spared and we went on our way unaware.

Janie:

Our family was granted the life saving miracle of my husband's unbelievable revival and recovery. A few years later my daughter was killed in a spectacular auto/semi-truck accident. We did not get the miracle of her life being spared. However in both events the small sustaining miracles were too many to recount here.

Miracles remind us we are never alone.

People on the outside looking in often remark or only notice the 'big' stuff. We as a people have to cultivate new eyes, miracle seeing eyes.

The saying "I cried because I had no shoes until I met a man who had no feet," has never been as meaningful as it is today. Most people are whiners. There is a national epidemic of 'rights.' People are screaming about their rights. When in fact there should be an epidemic of 'responsibilities.' The attitude among many is focused on what I don't have, what I can't do, or what I didn't get.

It is the "cat dish syndrome." Cats by nature are very contented animals. They entertain themselves in a myriad of ways with little concern of what is going on around them. Then the cat dish full of food appears. This is no problem unless there is more than one cat. For some reason a cat will eat itself sick rather than let the cat next to it eat more of the food. The cat forgets about the abundance of mice and other available vermin out in the field. Plenty of mice are out there for the cat to take at will. But, No... The only focus that cat has is the dish of food before it and how much the cat can and must consume before its rival cat eats the rest.

Janie:

One day I was full up with whining. I could not see anything good about my life. I had too many babies, too little sleep, too little money, too much work, too little help from my husband, etc. etc. I wanted a shoulder to cry on. I wanted sympathy. I called my Grandma Belle. I rehearsed all my troubles in elaborate detail to her. She listened carefully without much response. When I finished she said, "Is that it?"

"Uh, I guess so," I said a bit confused. I thought she would say something like, "Oh, you poor dear. Or I am so sorry you've got so many problems," or something else equally comforting.

"Well honey," Grandma Belle said, "as long as you are crying about all of that stuff you might as well have a really good cry over the fact that no matter how hard you try you are never going to be the Queen of England. I am so sorry but you just haven't got the right gene pool, so

if I were you, as long as you are in the crying mode, give that a good boohoo as well."

I started to laugh. "That is the silliest thing you have ever said."

"And so is everything you have just told me," Grandma Belle said. "Think about all the really great things in your life and stop your whining. It is stupid and it doesn't become you at all. There are just too many whiners out there. If you would stop whining and start looking, you would see miracles happening all around you. Why don't you think about those for a change? I think they will make you a whole lot happier."

Then she told me she had to go and hung up.

I was angry. I felt betrayed. Of all the people in the world I thought would understand how I felt I was sure it was Grandma Belle. What a put down she had given me. I started to cry. The babies were asleep and the older children had not come home from school yet.

We were living in a temporary rental in the canyon while we built a new home. I walked outside. It was early spring. Large granite boulders draped and shadowed here and there amongst the trees. The creek sprayed fresh renewal as it thundered against and through the river rocks. It crashed and thrashed, thriving on spring runoff. The breathtaking scenery was spectacular. A few patches of crusted snow lingered in spots. I walked up a secluded lane. Evidences of new life poked out of the spongy earth everywhere. I thought about Grandma Belle's words. "Stop whining and start looking."

The knot between my shoulders relaxed. Gratitude engulfed my soul. Being here in this canyon at this time was a miracle. My thoughts flooded with gratitude for all the real miracles of safety and health, children, a husband, food, a place to live, the beauty around me, and even my life itself. What did I really lack? I had everything essential.

In a few short weeks following this conversation Grandma Belle died from cancer. She was one of the truest miracle in my life. As she was *leaving this realm of existence she cared enough to show me how to live in it.*

Too many of us do not know how to 'live in it,' so our tendency is to whine over it.

It is a miracle you showed up at this time in this place. It is synchronicity. There is a reason. There is something for you to do that nobody else can do. You have a place here that nobody else can fill. When you are gone there will be a void, a space that can never be filled by anybody else. Somebody will know you have been here. You have a purpose. You are on a mission, a mission called life.

Everything in this life is here for us to use and enjoy, but we are not in charge. Just like a wise parent knows her little girl cannot eat too much candy or she will be sick, there are unseen caretakers watching over us. They know what we need. They know what will ultimately make us happy and what will make us sick… sick of heart, sick of body, sick of spirit. They know what we came here to learn. They are in charge. Things will happen on their timetable not ours.

We cannot control the circumstances of what is happening around us. We can only control our attitude.

Become Miracle Mavens. A maven is an expert, a connoisseur, mostly self-proclaimed. Proclaim yourself a Miracle Maven.

Janie:

I truly believe the greatest regrets each one of us will have as we exit this life will be… Why didn't I enjoy the journey more? Why did I stress so much over things that did not really matter? And how come I did not take time to see the miracles and be grateful?

Chapter 16 - End of Day, Shoes off, Feet up, Rest...

End of job... End of day... End of life.

We spend a lot of time, energy, and enthusiasm on new beginnings. Perhaps we do not give enough attention to the endings, as Paul Harvey said again and again, "The rest of the story."

In the end what do you want? When the day is over and you look back, what do you hope to see?

In our survey of women all over the world not one said she wanted to be remembered for some kind of corporate greatness. Every answer was some version of private introspection of that person's moral values.

For every beginning there will eventually be an ending. Most of the time we cannot predict what the outcome will be. Life is designed that way on purpose. There would be no surprises, no moments filled with wonderment and awe, no hope, and no reason to dream if we knew what was about to happen.

So if we cannot guarantee the results of our efforts, nor control the details of the journey, why contemplate the endings at all? Why not just leave them to fate and let the chips fall where they may?

Have you ever climbed to the top of a mountain? Even if you have made the trek before, this time will be different. You know the view will be worth the hike regardless of whether you have any idea or not of what you will see at the summit. The accomplishment of making it to the top will be the reward. The panoramic view is extra.

Although a person cannot accurately predict the eventual outcome of any particular event there are certain givens we can count on. If we plant snapdragon seeds it is unlikely we will reap a harvest of corn or tomatoes. The same idea is true for our lives. If we are prepared we need not fear. What we are prepared for rarely happens. If it does happen and we are ready for it then it is more of an inconvenience than a problem. It is the unexpected kicking us from behind that usually takes us down.

However, most of us do believe in living this day to the fullest magnitude possible. We believe it, but it is the doing it, that is so hard. Especially doing it with an eye to what future results our actions may engender.

To appreciate the view from the top of Joy Mountain, you have to put on those hiking shoes and start with the first step at the bottom of the hill. Then you must put one foot in front of the other until you finally reach the top.

For example: What if you want a higher standard of living with a better income? You will never get there if you are stuck flipping burgers and doing nothing else. You have to choose a job/profession of greater skill or education in some area of marketable expertise. And then you can flip burgers to pay for the schooling. You see… It is the reason behind why you are flipping burgers that counts.

Okay, so you also want a close relationship with your children, spouse, or friend. You must invest time in two things. Primarily spending time with the individual. And a close second is to understand the world around that person. This effort is all part of the trek.

Another word for all of this is sacrifice. What are you willing to give up now in order to have something better in the end?

To a great degree the actions we engage in today will determine the quality of our life and relationships tomorrow. In other words if you love bacon and tomato sandwiches made from summer ripe home grown tomatoes, make sure you have tilled and prepared the soil properly. And then, for heavens sake, plant it with tomatoes, not spaghetti squash. It takes a lot of time and patience to grow tomatoes. In August you cannot look up and say, "Oh dear, I really want some home grown tomatoes," and then run out, buy seeds, throw them in the ground and dump a summer's worth of water and fertilizer on top of them and expect that tomorrow you will have a thriving crop of tomatoes.

Ah, but what about the person who invests everything until her well of resources has dried up, parched, and cracked from lack of results? You did everything you were supposed to do and in the proper order, but for some reason this year's harvest was plagued with tomato worms, snails, grasshoppers, and draught.

Your child did not turn out the way you hoped.

You thought you would be secure financially by now, however, just paying the bills is still a struggle.

Where did all these health problems come from?

You were sure your husband would change, but you are still dealing with all the same issues.

Your forever marriage ended in divorce.

You did not get the promotion, that lack luster girl you work with got it instead.

Unfulfilled dreams, hopes, and desires, we have all got them. The question is what do we do with them?

Lyn:

I will be the first to admit that I am not good about throwing old shoes away. I gaze at a pair of brown loafers I purchased at Payless ten years ago. I never wear them anymore. I got my $7.95 out of them several times over, but occasionally I dust off the cobwebs and set them back on the shelf, just in case...

My rationalization, in regards to keeping the shoes, starts out demurely enough, but my imagination runs amuck getting bigger and better. Perhaps a homeless woman will knock on my door with holes in her shoes. I invite her in, feed her, and listen to her sad story of desertion by a cruel husband. I excuse myself and bring her the loafers. She, of course, is so grateful. Her eyes glisten with unshed tears and she tells me that she will never forget my kindness.

I smile at my fantasy knowing that the next time I wipe the cobwebs away I will make up a new story. The shoes will never be worn again unless I give them to good will.

I have memories in my life just like those loafers--old, cracked, worn-out experiences that need to be given away or burned. These are not good memories. Nor are they nice, snuggly reminisces that I would like to keep to go along with a cup of tea. These are memories, like those worn-out loafers--experiences that are uncomfortable, failures, disappointments, frustrations, and discouragements. There they are all gathering dust with an occasional spider taking up residency. These memories are commonly called baggage. And we all have some that we need to throw out with the trash.

Someone has said or done something that I just can't...won't forgive or forget. Or worse yet, I have offended someone I care about and now that I am over the initial anger, I can't seem to forgive myself.

Every time I walk into my closet I see those ugly brown loafers first. I pass by all the beautiful pairs of shoes--black, satin, sling backs for my son's wedding--a cute pair of sandals my daughter and I bought in Mexico. I even skim past the memory of my sweet husband hiring a rickshaw in Vietnam because I had worn sandals that were killing my feet and he refused to let me walk one more step until he found me a comfy pair of shoes.

I have so many good, loving memories, so why do I choose to dwell on the negative? That is what it is, isn't it, dwelling on the negative? In the movie Pretty Woman, Julia Robert's character says, "It's easier to believe the bad things about yourself."

Is it really? It may be easier, but it is much less painful the other way. Wouldn't we all be happier if we thought more about the positive memories in our lives and less about the negative ones? Isn't it time to take a rest from the energy it takes to harrow up all that old stuff? Isn't it time to find a better avenue for all the energy it takes to keep dusting off those old shoes?

And so you have come full circle. Here you are back at the beginning again, looking in that proverbial shoe closet of your life. Ask yourself… Have I learned anything along the way? Am I a little kinder? A little quieter? A little wiser? A little more grateful? A little bit more observant? A little stronger? A little healthier? A little happier?

Have you found which pair of shoes best serves your journey?

Put your feet up you deserve a rest? Just as God has given us new beginnings to try again and again and again to get it right, He has also given us endings. He knows we all need to rest now and again.

We are familiar with the end of the day, end of the school year, end of work, end of project, end of this book. Those are all obvious endings, however, there are lots of other resting points of renewal provided for us on this great journey of life.

Think about that marathon shopping excursion. You have walked a million miles and just when your feet are about to disconnect from your body you see a vacant chair or bench. As you off load your body and your bags, relief waves over you. Your feet can almost be heard saying out loud, "Thank you." You rest for a few minutes and then you offer up your seat to the next weary shopper. Now you are up and running again. But you had a rest.

It feels so good to sit down and rest for a minute.

Believe it or not the way to rest from stress is to work. This is different from "going to work." Working to rest from stress is a choice. You are choosing your work. Nobody is forcing you to do it. So immerse yourself in some project. Choose something that makes your muscles stretch, something that pushes you a bit harder than normal. Working in the yard is a good thing. Scrubbing the floor is another. Exert yourself. It doesn't necessarily cure the ill but it gives you renewed strength to cope. It gives you a rest.

Something physical is best because it incorporates more parts of your body and helps your body eliminate toxic elements that stressing stores up. It is the most effective rest for stress in the long term; however, attacking some kind of mental challenge can give you a rest from stress as well. Nursing homes have discovered that patients who engage themselves in challenging group games, or individual crossword puzzles, and other word or numbers exercises stay more alert, have less illness, and live longer. It takes their minds off the myriad of reasons they must live in this kind of a facility. They get a "rest."

Writing is another way to rest. Therapists know a patient can write down things they cannot seem to or do not want to express verbally. They dump out the garbage in their heads onto the paper and then they do not have to carry it around with them anymore. They get to rest. Writing engages your imagination. It is also a creative outlet. So is doodling. Writing or doodling for no good reason is restful. It gives you pause. When you go back to whatever, there is a sense of renewal, a sense of feeling rested.

Reading is also an activity that gives you a rest. Reading can take you places you have never been. You can be different people, do different jobs, and see different sights. It gives you a rest from whatever your immediate life has handed you.

When reading an intense novel the reader is grateful when the action pauses or the chapter ends. It gives the reader a chance to "rest" while staying involved in the story.

Our lives have moments when the action pauses as well. Maybe it happens when you catch a cold or the flu. You are forced to stop... to rest... to recuperate. Taking a minute to talk to a baby and then waiting for a response gives us a rest. It is also a kind of renewal. When the baby looks at us and mimics our antics it makes us smile. A smile gives us a rest. Laughing terminates the elements in our bodies that cause stress and illness. We get a rest from the toxic elements that attack us.

Having a pet can also relieve stress. The act of serving an animal and the animal serving you in return is rewarding in a way that gives rest to the soul. It is a non-threatening kind of unconditional love.

Janie:

My daughter, Sarah, came home every day, plopped her books on the table and played something on the piano before she did anything else. Everybody in the house could tell what kind of day she'd had by what she played. Music was her means of expression. It was her relief from stress. It was her rest.

After her death she communicated peace, a rest from the sorrow of her absence through music.

The morning after her death a dear neighbor got into his car to drive to work. Still distraught over the tragic events of the previous day, he turned on the radio. The DJ announced he was playing "an oldie but goodie." What crooned through the car speakers was a pop song from this man's teenage years that he had loved entitled 'Sarah'. He was stunned. He had not heard the song in years. He recounted later he felt that Sarah drove with him to work that morning. He was comforted and relieved of his anguish over her death. He felt rested.

Susan was Sarah's piano teacher. She played the prelude and postlude at Sarah's funeral service. She assembled a collection of appropriate religious and soft selections that were all Sarah's favorites. She told me she put all the music into a three ringed binder in no specific order and just began playing one piece after another about 20 minutes before the service was to start. She had no idea exactly when the family would be walking into the chapel since funerals are a little bit like weddings; they tend to have a timetable of their own.

As I entered the chapel Susan was playing "Watermark," by Enya. I recognized the piece and my whole body relaxed. My headache subsided. The tightness down the back of my neck released. Immediately I felt rested. This was my favorite song Sarah played in her after school choices. In my thoughts I heard Sarah say, "It's okay, Mom, I'm here don't be sad." Susan had no idea the significance this song held for me, but Sarah did.

Mary Ellen, Sarah's voice teacher, selected a medley of Sarah's favorite vocals to sing at the funeral. In the midst of this medley was an excerpt from Phantom of the Opera's "Think of Me." Family and friends commented that when Mary Ellen sang the words, "Think of me, think of me fondly, when I've said goodbye. Think of me once in awhile, please promise me you'll try," they felt Sarah was speaking right to each one of them. When they heard the words "and I will think of you..." they felt Sarah was telling them not to forget her and she would not forget them. It was a short respite from their sorrows.

The next Christmas my sister brought me a new CD of original Christmas songs. "Listen to this," she said, "and tell me if you don't think about Sarah." She continued. "It made me feel like Sarah was telling me Merry Christmas."

In the weeks following her death I had almost every person who had been close to Sarah come to me with an enthusiastic tale of some song speaking peace to them about Sarah. Most of them reported feeling Sarah's presence with them during those times.

It was a tender moment of rest for each person. An ending, a closure, it was the "rest" of the story.

Often we are unaware this is an ending. After all each day passes by but once. There is no dress rehearsal for life. We are on stage, under the lights, and before the audience, one time and only one time. When it's over it's over. We don't get to say, "Just kidding, let's do it again. I want to try it with more feeling, a different emphasis, or at a slower pace." This is the only chance you have. You get to be 33 years and 17 days old, only once, so you better make the most of it. Every day is important. Every day holds some kind of significance. Do not trivialize any day into oblivion.

Ralph Waldo Emerson said, "Write it in your heart that every day is the best day in the year."

Janie:

My mother jumped into her car and dashed over to my sister's house. She had lots of things on her mind. Thus being preoccupied, instead of driving into my sister's driveway, Mom drove into the driveway next door.

It was a familiar driveway. She had driven into it a hundred times before. It was the driveway of the house we all grew up in. When Mom realized what she had done, she chastised herself for being so absent minded. She had driven into this driveway out of a programmed habit from her past. A second later a wave of panic shuddered through her.

In this odd sense of fear she thought, "When was the last time I drove out of this driveway? I can't remember." Her brain shifted rapidly into historical rewind. She squeezed her thoughts trying to get it back. "This driveway was so much a part of everything about my life," she said to herself. "I drove in and out of it every day. How can I not remember the last time I drove away from this house?"

Sorrow overwhelmed her.

My mother had a perfectly wonderful house a few miles away from here. This house had served its purpose. When the time was right she had moved on to something that served a different purpose in her life.

She told me later. "In the brief minutes I sat in the forgotten driveway feeling stupid for landing in the wrong spot, I learned something important. If we realized all the endings we travel through each day we would be in a constant state of mourning. It would be like attending some kind of funeral over and over again."

Then she said, "Sometimes the gift is to not know, to not remember."

There are lots of things we need to throw out, things better off forgotten, and forgiven.

Do you have a ragged, dusty pair of brown loafers in your shoe closet of life that would serve you better in the trash? If so, burn em' baby' burn em'. Do not waste the precious space cluttering your life with things that need to be burned. Relieve yourself of all that unwanted past baggage and take a rest.

Forgive your children. Forgive your spouse. It does not matter if the spouse is a current or an ex, forgive him. Forgive your parents. Forgive your friends. Forgive your enemies. Forgive yourself. Then put up your feet and feel what it feels like to be rid of all that weight, what it feels like to rest.

Make your present moment count. You do not know (and probably it is a good thing) if you will never talk to this person again, never see this sight again, never have this experience, and never drive into this driveway again. It does not matter. You have your memory bank. Fill it with good things. Store it up with the kind of things you want to call back on a cold winter's eve sipping hot cocoa in front of a fire.

Focus on those treasured moments, the cherished memories, the hopes, and the dreams. Take a vacation from the world by dreaming about whatever is your perfect life. If you pretend long enough… who knows maybe you will find yourself living there.

End of day… sleep. Ahhhh the rest filled relief of sleep. Do not discount the importance of sleep. For years sleep was given little thought. It was a necessary evil. The body can only do so much and then it has to rest, so it goes to sleep. Sleep gives it the energy to go again. It is like a car needs both gas and oil to run properly. A body needs both nourishment and sleep. And that is about all the attention the world of science or anybody else gave to sleep.

Way back before modern technology a woman worked during the day while the sun was up. When the sun went down she could no longer work so she went to sleep until the sun came up again. It was simple. Nobody gave it much thought.

Times and technology have changed. The ability to work around the clock in conditions mimicking daylight is commonplace. The resulting affects of this phenomenon are not all positive. Sleep research has become a new avenue of scientific discovery. Sleepy drivers can be just as dangerous on the roads as drivers under the influence of drugs or alcohol. Sleep deprivation can lead to psychological problems, job related accidents, lack of performance in school, and health problems of every kind. Sleep apnea in a severe form can lead to heart attack, stroke, and death. A recent discovery involving sleep is about weight.

A lack of quality sleep can contribute to weight gain. And the newest information out is that increasing a person's sleep to between seven and eight hours can assist in shedding those unwanted pounds.

The pronouncements about the weight issues were so intriguing that Glamour Magazine decided to try their own independent study. Six women between 25 and 35 years of age made no other changes in their diet and exercise. The only thing they did was to maintain a regimen of seven and a half to eight hours of sleep a night for 10 weeks. One lady lost seven pounds, another nine, another six; another 10 pounds, another 12, and the winner lost a whopping 15 pounds. There are University studies supporting this information and provide all kinds of scientific backing about hormones, and enzymes, and nursery rhymes (not really nursery rhymes… just wanted to see if you were still reading) as the reasons why the body needs more sleep.

The bottom line is… we all need about seven to eight hours of sleep to nurture an optimum structure of health and well-being.

All aspects of our existence, our physical, emotional, and psychological self, need rest.

Resting is a time of retrospection as well as introspection. Hamlet said it well, "To sleep, to sleep, perchance to dream. Aye, there's the rub…" In other words the problem with sleep is we think too much while we are doing it. If we feel guilty, or inadequate, or ashamed, or bad in any other sense whether justified or not, it all interferes with our sleep.

Aside from seeking professional help, which we encourage you to do if you have major problem with your sleep, sleep patterns, or general health, there are some simple things you may try to ease yourself into the sleep mode:

Don't eat after 7:00 p.m.

Don't drink alcohol after 7:00 pm.

Don't watch movies or programs that make your adrenaline surge just before going to sleep.

Make sure your room is dark.

If you must get up by a specific time, set an alarm. Often a person finds herself waking up every hour or so to check the time. Let the clock take that responsibility.

Let it go… whatever 'it' is. Imagine yourself setting your problem on the shelf where you can pick it up again tomorrow.

Count as you breathe. As you inhale count slowly until your lungs are full. Hold your breath for the same count as you reached while breathing in. Exhale to the same number of counts. Continue this activity as long as possible. Block out thoughts of anything else. Concentrate only on breathing and counting. This is a very simple but effective form of meditation.

Use meditation or other quiet forms of release at bedtime to calm your muscles and prepare the body for sleep.

Believe it or not warm milk, sometimes in the form of hot chocolate, a light warm custard, or certain herbal teas specially blended for nighttime and sleeping, can help.

Establish a mantra, something you repeat over and over that blocks out your unwanted thoughts. This mantra should be something that leaves you feeling positive and hopeful.

The shoe closet is clean. You have thrown out the junk and run a mile. You have discounted the well-meaning opinions of others and you no longer make negative assumptions and judge other people and their circumstances. What a relief. You feel rested already.

You have also stepped outside of the comfort zone of your shoebox and dumped your guilt. Your lists and journals are meaningful tools instead of manifests of self-defeating failure.

After a bit of trial and error you have found your quiet spot and retreat there often. You have become sponge-like in absorbing information floating around you and allow your imagination free rein in solving life's problems and dilemmas.

Nature is now your battery recharge location. A renewed awareness of the world invigorates you and you courageously offer your assistance and help out when a need arises. You don't have to be told what to do anymore your eyes are open and you see more things on your own.

Gratitude and God walk hand in hand with you on this incredible journey. And you are open to the possibility of angels trekking along the path and clearing stumbling stones in your way.

You have found true Joy in your Journey.

Even if you had lots of joy before, this book has enhanced it for you. And look… it is truly a miracle you have come to the end of the book and you are still here.

Lyn and Janie thank you for taking the time to read, to listen, and to consider the possibilities. They have discovered these things make their journey of life more enjoyable, rewarding, and just plain fun.

May you always find Joy in your journey no matter where it takes you.

Every now and then when you might have forgotten something we said, or you need a lift, pick up this book again and…

Sit back. Take your shoes off. Put your feet up, and rest.

The End

Janie Van Komen...

Janie Van Komen survived the untimely death of her sixteen-year-old daughter, her husband's massive heart attack at age forty-seven that left them financially depleted with ten children to support, losing several million dollars, bankruptcy, being evicted from her home, recovering from a shattered leg and ankle, and a myriad of other bizarre events to become a much sought after speaker.
Both youth and adult groups seek her formula of finding joy in the journey. Janie infuses both laughter and tears into empowering teaching moments and making the trek a little easier for all. Although technically Janie and husband, Robert, only have their youngest son, Ben living with them at the moment, her house is constantly filled with the comings and goings of her ten children, their spouses, and 35 grands.

Lyn Austin...

Lyn Austin is currently a published author with Boroughs Publishing. She traveled the world lecturing for cruise lines, including; Royal Caribbean, Celebrity, and Disney. She is a member of the American Business Women and willingly shares her secrets of success with others.

Rising above severe obesity, the bizarre accidental death of her first husband, subsequent financial, health, and relationship devastations, Lyn emerged with an attitude of gratitude, a newfound confidence and an infectious passion for life. She hosts uplifting retreats helping women in all walks of life. Lyn lives on the edge of the Snake River with husband, Butch.

She and Butch together have six married children and 20 grandchildren.

www.ingramcontent.com/pod-product-compliance
Lightning Source LLC
Chambersburg PA
CBHW022102160426
43198CB00008B/318